THE MANAGEMENT OF CHANGE——

THE MANAGEMENT
OF CHANGE————————

Administrative Logics and Actions

Joseph W. Weiss————————————

PRAEGER

New York
Westport, Connecticut
London

Library of Congress Cataloging-in-Publication Data

Weiss, Joseph W.
  The management of change.

  Bibliography: p.
  1. Vocational rehabilitation – United States – History –
20th century.   2. Sheltered workshops – United States –
History – 20th century.   3. Organizational change.
4. Strategic planning.   I. Title.
HD7256.U5W38   1986   658.4   86-9390
ISBN 0-275-92195-6 (alk. paper)

Library of Congress Catalog Card Number: 86-9390
ISBN: 0-275-92195-6

First published in 1986

Praeger Publishers, 521 Fifth Avenue, New York, NY 10175
A division of Greenwood Press, Inc.

Printed in the United States of America

The paper used in this book complies with the Permanent
Paper Standard issued by the National Information Standards
Organization (Z39.48-1984).

10 9 8 7 6 5 4 3 2 1

To Hayat and Taya

Preface

Studies dealing with the management of political, cultural, and economic change in and around organizations have generally not described executive and coalitional strategies or policy outcomes. Literature on leadership and strategy abounds with prescriptions and models for identifying alignments between management styles and environmental conditions, but these paradigms often tend to be vague and uninteresting. Issues relating to power and politics have been almost completely overlooked. The recent dominance of deterministic theories and positivistic methodologies in organizational literature has contributed to the proliferation of static models for studying leadership and environmental change.

This study is an exploratory attempt to describe and examine the observed relationships among three individual administrators' strategies and changing environmental conditions characterized as growth, critical turbulence, and cutback. These are state vocational rehabilitation administrators in what has been one of the country's most progressive organizations in this industry. The games they played, and the political tactics and strategies they used are part of the strategy implementation process on which we have concentrated.

The intended contribution of this study is aimed at reviving classical and contemporary theoretical action perspectives that have paved the way for studying executive strategy-making and implementation activities. The scholarly works of Selznick and Chandler, in particular, seem to have been either lost or neglected in this area. Also, the works of the French sociologist Lucien Karpik, and of Graham Allison have not been extensively used to examine the policy implementation process of executives in public sector organizations.

If this work generates interest in the development and use of these and other action research strategies for studying the strategic management of change, our purpose will have been served.

Acknowledgments

I wish to thank Michael Aiken, André Delbecq, Cora Marrett, and Richard Schoenherr for their suggestions and criticisms on a previous work on which this study was based. While this author assumes all responsibility for the content of this book, I express my gratitude to these individuals for their help in shaping the theory and structure of the work.

I am also grateful to those people in the organization who remain anonymous here but whose participation in this study was significant. The time they gave in numerous interviews and informal conversations made this possible.

Also, to Dean John Burns and my colleagues in the Management Department of Bentley College I extend thanks for their encouragement and support of the completion of this project.

To Mary Trimble, our word processing supervisor, I offer a special tribute. I am one of the countless people whose careers she continues to help. Also, I thank Diane Viveiros for her word processing assistance.

The publishers at Praeger must be recognized for their patience and expertise, which guided my efforts in getting the manuscript into book form.

Finally, I wish to thank my friends and family—Hayat, my wife, my daughter, Taya, and my mother. Their support is responsible for a large part of this product.

Contents

List of Tables and Figure

TABLE

TABLE

FIGURE

Introduction

A PROCESS RESEARCH AGENDA

Organizational research examining the process of strategy formulation and policy implementation has omitted or minimized the intentionality, power, and influence of the organizational actors in general and of top-level leaders particularly (Selznick 1957; Child 1972; Benson 1977; Karpik 1972b). As a result, the impact of powerful organizational actors' strategic decisions in negotiating policy has not been examined. Studies in this field also have not systematically identified or linked the dominant strategies of particular organizational leaders to relevant external political, economic, and legal constraints or to groups with which administrators negotiate policy (Karpik 1978, 1972b; MacMillan 1978; Hambrick 1981). Consequently, organizational research has been uninformative about the sources and relationships of power within and between the policy-implementing organization and groups in the political environment. Thus, the following research questions have not been addressed because they have not been considered problematic:

●Whose goals are implemented into actual policy?
●What is the political process internal and external to the implementing organization in which strategy is conceived and formulated?
●What are the mechanisms the implementing agency's leadership uses to manipulate, control, and negotiate its interests into policy?

- What are the structural constraints external to the organization that influence and are affected by the leaders' strategic choices?
- What are the differences between intended strategies and objectives of organizational leaders as these are constructed from observed policy outcomes?
- Under what historical and environmental conditions are individually observed leadership implementation and control strategies and styles more successful in enacting policies?

These questions assume a purposive and political view of an organization's leaders. However, because research in this area has been dominated by conceptually limited perspectives, analysts have generally treated strategy either as a "situational art, an imaginative act of integrating numerous complex decisions" (e.g., the Harvard Business School's normative approach as exemplified by Andrews 1971) or as "disjointed, incremental decisions made in reaction to pressing problems without overall integration among decisions over time" (Lindblom 1959). Neither of these dominant perspectives used to study organizational strategy offers an adequate framework for systematically linking observed individual CEO strategic choices to implemented policy. In fact, there is a continuing discussion among theorists in the field of organizational strategy over the following major issues:

1. What is a meaningful definition of strategy that can be operationalized and measured (Schendel and Hofer 1979)?
2. Do organizational members actually develop strategies (Quinn 1977)?
3. Are organizational strategies both intentionally and unintentionally chosen and pursued (Mintzberg 1978)?
4. Should the concept of strategy include ends (objectives) and means (methods of achieving desired ends) (Schendel and Hofer 1979)?
5. What are the conceptual linkages between strategy and social values (Gallie 1978; Hage and Dewar 1973), organizational structure (Stopford and Wells 1972; Chandler 1969), performance (Hatten and Schendel 1979), organizational processes like planning and control (Mintzberg 1973; Miles and Snow 1978), and environmental factors?

Organizational theorists, with the exception of certain historical studies (Allison 1971; Stone 1974; Edwards 1977; Goldman and Van Houten 1980), continue to view organizational strategy from a static systems perspective, which conceptualizes effective combinations between nonhistorical, environmental dimensions and nonvolitional, internal organizational properties (Miles and Snow 1978; Thompson 1967; Lawrence and Lorsch 1967). The result of these efforts has been a sociologically uninteresting and unrealistic portrayal of organizational strategy and policy as adaptive extensions of nonvolitional social actors.

This chapter reviews the literature that emphasizes a view of the organization as a political system whose leaders are responsible for selecting and implementing policy choices. Before examining this literature, a definition of organizational leadership as used in this study is offered below.

Theoretical Foundation for Studying
Administrative Leadership

Burns and Stalker (1961) indicate that senior organizational administrators and officials control the initiation and implementation of policy regardless of size and technical experience required to run a large, sophisticated organization. Selznick (1957), Karpik (1978), and Chandler (1969) also argue that individual, powerful organizational leaders formulate strategies that determine the structure and policy of firms. Leadership in this study refers to the top-level administrative executive and his/ her dominant coalition of the organization, which is invested with the power, status, and resources to manipulate, interpret, and negotiate constraints and resources into policy. The extent to which individual executives share and delegate their power and influence with internal and external organizational members and groups (for example, with a dominant coalition) in their strategy-making activities varies. Reconstructing the strategic logic and the resultant policy outcomes reveals those with whom the leader actually shared power to enact particular strategies.

The conceptual basis of the activities top-level administrators pursue is based on Katz and Kahn's (1978) discussion of leadership behavior. They state (1978:536) that top-level organizational leaders: use existing structure to administer and operate the organization efficiently; improvise organizational structure to adapt to environmental change; and introduce structural change to formulate policy. The primary interest in this study is in the third area of activity, policy formulation. Katz and Kahn state that the power and authority over this organizational activity belong to the top-level organizational leaders, for example, "Except in democratically constituted systems, only the top echelons of line and staff officers are really in a position to introduce change in structure" (1978:537).

In this study Katz and Kahn's conceptual activity of policy implementation is extended to include an examination of intended as well as realized dominant leadership strategies and the effects on structure and policy outcomes. To formulate and enact major policy, organizational leaders must manipulate external and internal groups, constraints, and demands. To understand the dominant control strategies leaders actually use to manipulate intraorganizational arrangements and to enact particular policy, it is necessary to identify and distinguish the intended from the observed leadership strategies (means) and outcomes (ends). Establishing the relationship between these dimensions enables the researcher to understand the actual process as well as the implemented result of executives' strategic choices. This research effort is the first step toward comparative analysis aimed at determining the alignments between environments and successful strategies.

Leadership Literature: Two Divergent Views

A review of the organizational literature on leadership theory reveals a difference of opinion over the importance of the strategic role of top-level executives and the substantive impact of their strategies on organizational policy. This divergence is due to two views of executive leadership: the first contends that a leader's actions are insignificant in determining organizational policy. Proponents include organizational theorists representing the following perspectives: the natural selection model (Aldrich 1972; Aldrich and Pfeffer, 1976), the resource dependency perspective (Pfeffer 1977, 1981; Pfeffer and Salancik 1978), and the "garbage can" and "organized anarchy" perspectives (Cohen and Olsen 1972).

The second view holds that executives shape and implement organizational policy. The role of leaders is critical, according to this view, in formulating strategy that is translated into major policy outcomes. This school comprises different theorists who share research assumptions about the importance of leadership in impacting on policy (Selznick 1957; Chandler 1969; Child 1972; Katz and Kahn 1978; and Lucien Karpik 1978). A presentation of the assumptions and arguments of the first view is discussed and criticized first.

The Determinist Perspective of Pfeffer and Salancik: Leadership as Myth and Symbol

Proponents of the resource dependency perspective argue that the strategic role of leaders in organizations is insignificant

in determining policy. Theorists of this perspective recognize
the importance of top-level organizational leaders as symbols.
Leadership is associated with myths socially constructed to
legitimate role occupants (Pfeffer 1977).

Pfeffer and Salancik (1978:9,10) state the following three
theoretical arguments for "expecting that individuals would
have less effect on organizational outcomes than would an organization's context": first, personal and organizational processes
lead to similarity among organizational leaders; "this means that
there is a restriction on the range of skills, characteristics,
and behaviors of those likely to achieve positions of importance
in organizations" (1978:9). Second, Pfeffer and Salancik contend
that when a top-level position in an organization is achieved,
discretion to make decisions is limited. Finally, these organizational theorists argue that many actions and events that affect
organizational outcomes are not controlled by organizational
members. As examples, they cite the economic cycle, tariffs,
regulations, and tax policies for businesses; for school districts
they cite budgets, legislative actions, and other external factors.

Pfeffer refers to social psychological literature (Berscheid
and Walster 1969) to illustrate the ineffectiveness of leaders
based on the biased organizational selection process. "The
attraction literature," he states, "suggests that there is a
tendency for persons to like those they perceive as similar"
(1977:375). Pfeffer generalizes these research findings to an
organizational selection process, contending that leaders are
homogeneous in their skills and perceptions because they are
selected by persons with similar preferences, backgrounds,
and abilities. The result is ineffectiveness in leadership performance at the highest organizational level.

Pfeffer also argues that the selection of organizational
leaders is overly constrained by the internal influence system
in organizations. These constraining factors lead to leadership
ineffectiveness and inability to effect individual strategic choices.
Pfeffer and Salancik's study (1978) of hospital administrators
is used to demonstrate the influence of the organizational context on leadership selection. They found that there is a relationship between tenure of hospital administrators and the hospital
context.

Finally, to illustrate the overconstraining influence of the
external environment on leadership behavior, Pfeffer alludes
to Lieberson and O'Connor's study (1972) of 167 business firms
in 13 industries over a 20-year period in which they found the
effects of changes in the top executive position to have had a
limited effect on organizational outcomes (e.g., sales, profits,
and profit margins) compared to economic conditions, type of
industry, and company effects.

From these arguments and research findings, Pfeffer is led to a strategy for studying organizational leadership that essentially separates the leader from strategy formulation and policy implementation activities. "Considering all these factors," he states, "it is not likely administrators would have a large effect on the outcomes of most organizations" (1977:10).

It should be noted that Pfeffer has more recently (1981) recognized and discussed the issue of power in the decision-making activities of organizational elites; however, his theoretical discussion is limited to a static view of top-level leaders' behavior, which is viewed within an adaptive conceptual framework of organizations. This framework emphasized environmental constraints and resources as independent causal processes acting on a leaders' decisions. Pfeffer states, "Change in organizations is largely externally induced, and that to the extent that the organization successfully buffers or insulates itself from the environment, change is forestalled" (1981:331). Such a conceptual framework views the role of organizational leaders as adaptive, defensive, and isolating. Again, Pfeffer reasons, "exactly what makes insulation and buffering so desirable for those in the organization's dominant coalition—they can assure their continued control for a longer period of time to the extent that they can succeed in isolating the organization from its environment" (1981:331).

Aldrich: Leadership as Externally Controlled. Aldrich, a proponent of the natural selection model of organizations, views the role of leaders in a manner similar to the position held by Pfeffer and Salancik, namely that the impact of leaders on environmental constraints is minimal. A major difference, however, is that Aldrich leaves the possibility open for leaders of the largest and most powerful corporations to effectively impact external constraints under certain conditions. His position can be summarized as follows:

> While strategic choice is possible under certain conditions, I will argue that because of the powerlessness of most organizations, barriers to choice because of interorganizational dependence, and problems in perception and information processing, the opportunities for strategic choice are severely limited. (1978:136)

Also similar to Pfeffer and Salancik's arguments, Aldrich reasons that

Environmental selection processes set the limits
within which rational selection among alternatives
takes place. Prior limits and constraints on available options leave little room for maneuvering by
most organizations, and strategic choice may be a
luxury open only to the largest and most powerful
organizations. (1978:160)

Aldrich's conclusions as stated above are based on the
following three major arguments: first, there are constraints
on the "capacity of decision makers to make optimal choices of
new environmental niches"; second, there are limits on the
power of organizations to affect or influence their environments;
and third, there are limits to organizational participants' perceptions of reality and environments in making strategic choices
(1978:149).

The first argument focuses on legal and cost barriers.
The point is that potential environments may be excluded because of these constraining factors. The second argument is
also based on the prohibitive costs and legal barriers which
exclude smaller, less powerful organizations from impacting on
their environment.

Aldrich acknowledges the power of "the 6 percent of
corporations with assets over one million dollars or the 11 percent
with sales over one million dollars" that dominate many aspects
of "life in the United States" (1978:154). He continues to argue,
however, that "the issue we must address . . . is whether it
is fruitful to build a sociology of organizations on exceptional
organizations."

The third argument he advances emphasizes the social
forces that "limit the possibility for really 'strategic' choices"
since individuals' perceptions of the environment are imperfect.
Aldrich relies on Starbuck's discussion (1976) about the constraining environmental factors that limit choice. He also uses
selected social psychological studies (Festinger 1954; Taijfel
1969) when arguing this point.

Cohen, March, and Olsen: Leadership as Random Process.
Other organizational theorists who argue against the importance
of leaders' impact on policy are proponents of the "garbage
can" and "organized anarchy" models of organizations (Cohen
and Olsen 1972). The arguments of these theorists are
based primarily on studies of universities and university presidents. These models deny the intentionality of organizational
members in making strategic decisions. The theorists stress

instead situational factors, habit, and custom. As Cohen and
Olsen have stated (1972:26), "In a garbage can situation, a
decision is an outcome of an interpretation of several relatively
independent 'streams' within an organization." Streams refer
to solutions, problems, participants, and decision opportunities.
The number of organizational actors, choices, problems, and
solutions complicates the problem-solving process to the extent
that individual actors tend to deal with selected decisions. For
example, Cohen and Olsen (1972:37) state that

> events are not dominated by intention. The processes
> and the outcomes are likely to appear to have no
> close relation with the explicit intention of actors.
> In situations in which load is heavy and the structure
> is relatively unsegmented, intention is lost in context
> dependent flow of problems, solutions, people and
> choice opportunities.

These theorists also argue that individual members' actions
in organizations precede their preferences (March 1978). Members actually know what they have done only after the action
has occurred. Following this logic, individual and collective
goals of organizational actors become retrospective rationaliza-
tions of preceding actions. The emphasis is on unintentional
and unplanned activities and strategies of organizational members.
In such a model of decision-making activities, policy outcomes are explained as random events without any intentional
strategies of level and leaders may, according to these authors,
serve an important symbolic and mythical function for the
organization; they are viewed as powerless to manipulate environmental contingencies, resources, and constraints for their
or the organization's ends; and powerless to guide and control
intraorganizational politics and decision-making activities toward
desired predetermined ends.
Proponents of these organizational perspectives view
explicitly or by inference top-level organizational leaders as
nonvolitional, unintentioned role players whose primary objectives are to buffer and insulate the organization from environmental forces.
Research findings that support the theoretical bases of
these proponents' views of organizational leadership are limited
in the majority of cases to social psychological and to cross-
sectional, self-reported statistical surveys of mid-level supervisory managers. Such findings have been generalized and/or
imputed to top-level organizational administrators.

The Strategic Choice Perspective

The second contrasting view of organizational leadership consists of theorists (Selznick 1957; Chandler 1969; Child 1972; Katz and Kahn 1978; Karpik 1978) who argue for the dominant role leaders play in formulating and directing strategy for the entire organization. A summary of the major theoretical assumptions and findings of these analysts follows below.

Katz and Kahn: Requirements of Purposive Leadership. Katz and Kahn (1978:528) argued that the "essence of organizational leadership was the influential increment over and above mechanical compliance with the routine directives of the organization. Such an influential increment derives from the fact that human beings rather than computers are in positions of authority and power."

Katz and Kahn present five basic reasons why organizations need leadership at the top level. First, organizations are incomplete in their formal design, charter, and written policies, especially as these are compared to the "ongoing cycles of behavior that define the pattern of the 'real' organization" (1978:532). According to this analysis, the actual behavior of organizational participants is "infinitely more complex, inclusive and variable" than any formal plan or organizational chart. Also, the formal organizational plan, if taken literally by participants, would lead to a form of "legal insubordination and sabotage." Following the letter of the law would not get critical work accomplished. Leadership is therefore needed because "the concrete case always needs something of interpretation and adaptation, embellishment or thoughtful omission" (1978:532).

Second, top-level leadership is needed in organizations for boundary-spanning functions. Because the relationship between the organization's subsystems and the environment are never specified according to programmed arrangements, "leadership emerges as individuals take charge of relating a unit or subsystem to the external structure or environment. Where no formal role has been designated for a leader, an informal one arises especially for those at juncture points in the system (1978:532).

A third argument for the need of organizational leadership is that for "invention and creativity beyond the performance of role requirements" in managing environmental demands. "Since this environment is subject to technological, legal, cultural, climatic, and many other kinds of change, the organization is characteristically confronted with demands that it change too . . . or establish a new relationship on the terms now available" (1978: 533). This function of leaders, adjusting the organization to environmental demands or creating new organizational structures, requires "leadership of a high order."

Fourth, organizational leaders are needed to continually coordinate the internal dynamics and staff of organizations that face change. "The result of such internal differences and organizational tendencies is not merely a continuing need for coordination and adjudication. It is persisting organizational change, internally and in relation to the environment, and a consequent need for additional complementary changes, in order to achieve a new balance and working structure" (1978:534). Leadership is especially needed when organizations extend their control over environments by adding new functions. Consequently, the need arises for adopting new policies and structures.

Finally, organizational leaders are needed in order to adapt the rewards, penalties, and work content of the people who change an organization. Katz and Kahn argue that "only people can be members of an organization, but people are not only members of organizations, and above all not members of only one organization. . . . These extraorganizational and other-organizational aspects of a person's life affect behavior of the person in the organization" as well as the person's job and the organization (1978:534).

Katz and Kahn discuss three major types of leadership activities in organizations: policy formulation, the piecing (interpolation) of the existing structure to operate the organization effectively, and the use of the present organizational structure to run the organization. They contend that these three activities call for "different cognitive styles, different degrees and types of knowledge and different affective characteristics" (1978:538). The activity of policy formulation, in particular, requires abilities and skills that cognitively suggest a total system perspective, as well as charisma. The organizational level to which this leadership activity (with accompanying skills) applies is that of "top echelons" (1978:539):

> The formulation of policy and the origination of
> structure represents the kind of leadership acts
> most appropriate to charismatic leadership. The
> great majority of people are not in a position to
> evaluate proposals for major organizational change
> in any detail. They may or may not want to see
> social changes, and they may be sound in their

judgement of overall goals, but they will not often
be knowledgeable about specific programs to attain
these goals. Hence they will turn to the great
leader whose character, strength, and skill give
assurance that the problem will be solved. (1978:546)

Katz and Kahn's recognition of the critical activities and
functions of individual top-level organizational leaders revives
a theoretical interest in an area that has been neglected for
over two decades of organizational research, especially since
Selznick's 1957 work on leadership.

Selznick: Leadership as Institutional Statesmanship. Selznick's
theoretical statement on organizational leadership (1957) remains
a landmark in the field. His essay represents a cogent argument against research and theory preoccupied with administrative
and organizational efficiency to the exclusion of the role of
individual top-level leaders in formulating and implementing
policy. Katz and Kahn (1978:543) have summarized Selznick's
contribution on the subject as follows:

Among theorists of leadership, the importance of
systematic perspective, external and internal, has
been best recognized and explicated by Selznick
(1957). It is at the heart of his distinction between
institutional leadership and mere administrative
efficiency.
For Selznick, the institutional leader is the
unique possessor of system perspective, and it is
this quality which distinguishes him or her from
the leader who is merely an interpersonal adept.
Institutional leaders are concerned with policies
as well as with persons; they are concerned with
content as well as with process. . . . There may
be only two or three decisions in the course of a
year that demand perspective on this level, but
Selznick argues that they are crucial.

Selznick stated his purpose (1957:4) for writing on organizational leadership as follows:

The argument of this essay is quite simply stated:
The executive becomes a statesman as he makes the
transition from administrative management to institutional leadership. This shift entails a reassessment

of his own tasks and of the needs of the enterprise
. . . it means viewing the organization as an institution.

This statement is important in that Selznick distinguishes
leadership in organizations from management, and views the
organization as an institution. The tasks of the leadership will
be discussed after Selznick's concept of the organization as an
institution is clarified.

For Selznick an institution was a "product of social needs
and pressures" (1957:5). Viewing organizations as institutions
meant understanding the social, political, and historical context
of the organization. An institutional analysis of an organization
for Selznick entailed the study of "more general connections
between policy and social structure." He states, "Administrative
issues will be decided only after a diagnosis that takes account
of the historical context" (1957:103).

Selznick, then, centers the study of leadership within the
external historical and political context of the organization. He
proceeds to examine the critical tasks of leaders in their policymaking activities.

It is in the realm of policy—including the areas
where policy-formation and organization-building
meet—that the distinctive quality of institutional
leadership is found. . . . it is the function of the
leader-statesman—whether of a nation or a private
association—to define the ends of group existence,
to design an enterprise distinctively adapted to
these ends, and to see that that design becomes
a living reality. These tasks are not routine;
they call for continuous self-appraisal on the part
of the leaders; and they may require only a few
critical decisions over a long period of time.
(1957:37)

Selznick's theoretical orientation on institutional leadership
is also distinctive in that he explicitly states that one important
function of leaders is to "choose key values and to create a
social structure that embodies them" (1957:61). Leaders are
responsible for maintaining the internal organizational structure,
then, as well as directing policy externally. The critical tasks,
as opposed to routine functions, that leaders must accomplish
according to Selznick include the definition of the institutional
mission and role; deciding on the means to achieve the ends

desired; representing the institutional embodiment of purpose defending the organization's integrity; and ordering internal conflict.

According to Selznick, "The leader's job is to test the environment to find out which demands can become truly effective threats, to change the environment by finding allies and other sources of external support, and to gird his organization by creating the means and the will to withstand attacks" (1957: 145).

However, as McNeil (1978) observed, Selznick's arguments and methods were "greatly influenced by the heavy functionalist interpretation he placed on these organizational dynamics. Seeing the ultimate functional need as organizational survival, he felt that each organization would develop a very unique pattern of adaptation and control." McNeil (1978) also contended that had Selznick focused on the "dynamics of struggle" between the focal organizational leaders and the external market context instead of the "one best way" that leaders could protect the organization in adapting to environmental pressures, Selznick's theoretical arguments would be more powerful in understanding organizational and societal relationships.

Nevertheless, Selznick's theoretical contributions form a groundwork for constructing a perspective on leaders as powerful actors whose key strategies and implementation mechanisms can impact on environmental groups and organizations. Although his analytical framework is couched in adaptive and survivalist language, his basic concepts of the organization as an historically and societally centered institution, of the leader as a purposive statesman who is responsible for nonroutine, critical tasks, and his focus on linking the policymaking activities of leaders to environmental forces and internal organizational structure, all contribute to a view of organizational and leadership activities as being beyond efficiency concerns to include political dimensions of activities and strategies.

Chandler: Structure Follows Leadership Strategies. In addition to the works of Selznick and Katz and Kahn, Chandler's historical study (1969) of the expansion of dominant U.S. industries at the turn of the century also offers evidence to support a purposive and political view of individual top-level organizational leaders.

Chandler's thesis, as documented by historical comparative records, is that the chief executive officer as leader formulates strategy for the organization. Once formed and implemented, the structure of the firm follows the directives and plan of the strategy. Chandler's findings went against the direction of organizational research for at least two decades following his study.

Chandler's study focused on the last two decades of the nineteenth century, a time when U.S. industrial firms were rapidly expanding. Industrial expansion continued after 1900 because of the rapid growth of urban population and technological advances. The largest, most powerful industries met the new needs and opportunities of the growing economy and the expanding technological advances by developing three strategies. These were the result of the individual executives. The strategies included expanding the firm's existing line to new customers by searching for new markets and sources of supply in foreign countries or by opening new markets by developing new products for different types of customers.

Those industries that continued making the same products for the same customers faced few new types of administrative problems and were run through older, centralized, functional departmentalized structures. Industries most affected by new markets and technologies solved their expansion problems by diversifying their organizational structures. The multidivisional organization structure was the response to this development. This new structure was a conscious and planned strategy of the executives. Chandler relates how engineering training, rational and analytical problem-solving approaches to strategy-making, combined with youthful leaders who had a relatively short incumbency in any one position, all helped administrators become innovators in formulating and implementing strategic decisions.

Chandler's study also demonstrated the independent effects top-level strategy had on organizational structure. He showed that the background, training, and problem-solving abilities of executives were decisive in their capacity to successfully evaluate and select strategies that met the environmental demands placed on organizations. The results of his study evidence the continuing need to examine not only the strategies executive administrators choose, but to study the executives' backgrounds and skills in decision making.

Chandler's is a historical study. This method of research has been neglected in recent years in favor of statistical and survey methods. Consequently, the environmental factors that impinge on an executive's perceived and observed need to change the organization's structure have not been systematically studied.

Child: Leadership as Political Process. In the same conceptual camp as Katz and Kahn, Selznick, and Chandler is John Child.

Child's perspective emphasizes the political role of powerful organizational leaders (he chose to use the concept of dominant coalition) in making strategic choices. His theoretical model outlines the process a dominant coalition undergoes in developing strategy:

> the first stage . . . is the coalition members' evaluation of their organization's position—what expectations are presented by resource providers such as business shareholders, what is the trend of events in the environment, what has been the organization's recent performance, the congeniality of its present internal configuration. . . . Their prior ideology is assumed to colour this evaluation in some degree.

Then,

> The choice of goals or objectives for the organization is seen to follow on from this evaluation, and to be reflected in the strategic action which is decided upon. (1972:17)

According to this particular model, the outcomes of the strategic choice are considered internal organizational arrangements, structure, and particular external consequences of the action taken, such as a move into or out of given markets or areas of activity. Also of importance in this model is Child's notion of performance, which he defines as an informational input to the dominant coalition.

Child also points out that his theoretical orientation is relevant to all work organizations.

> "Work organizations" are defined as those within which work is carried out on a regular basis by paid employees, and which have been deliberately established for explicit purposes. The category includes organizations with formal objectives as diverse as business enterprises, hospitals, educational institutions, government departments and the administrative offices of trade unions. An assumption underlying much available research . . . is that the engagement in systematic work and exchange which characterizes all these types, provides a basis for comparison within a common theoretical framework. (1972:2)

Child's particular concern with these diverse types of organizations is an important contrast both to Perrow's (1963) call for the study of powerful, "nontrivial" organizations and to Aldrich's (1979) claim that Child's political orientation on strategic choice is applicable only to the largest corporations. Child's contention is that the leadership's dominant strategies in all "work organizations" are subject to examination in determining the effects of these strategies on the internal organizational structure and on its implemented policies.

Child's theoretical orientation is partially derived from such studies as Chandler (1969), Cyert and March (1963), Normann (1969) and Bain (1959). These studies, according to Child, share the common assumption that "organizational decision-makers do take positive steps to define and manipulate their own corners of the environment" (1972:9). These studies have shown too that "the relationships between organization and environment are variable . . . the most important aspect of these relationships concerns the degree of influence which the controllers of one organization can exert over their counterparts in other organizations" (1972:10).

Karpik: The Logics of Action of Leaders. Under the second view presented here on the purposive role of top-level leaders is a discussion of the French organizational sociologist Lucien Karpik. In particular, Karpik's works taken together (1972a, 1972b, 1972c, 1972d, 1978) represent a single comprehensive framework for examining goal-attainment activities of organizational administrative elites. In the discussion that follows, Karpik's image of the organization, his basic unit of analysis, and his concept of logics of action (strategies) is briefly summarized in order to emphasize his view of the organization as a political arena of powerful actors.

Influenced by Cyert and March (1963), Karpik views the organization as a loosely coupled political system in which individuals who are motivated by private interests form coalitions. These coalitions bargain and compete for power and position in order to enforce their own ends over the organization. A dominant coalition emerges from these internal struggles. This coalition may be composed of top-level leaders and other members of the firm. This leadership controls the resources of the organization and uses them to achieve its own ends. These ends may or may not be those of the wider organization.

Karpik's basic unit of analysis is the individual organizational actor. Individual actors, however, become associated with coalitions who in turn are members of the particular firm, which is part of an industrial group, which also is part of the national economy that is linked to the world market. These relationships are interwoven into a complex set of political, economic, and social interactions that, according to Karpik, can be separated and studied only from a bottom-up approach; that is, it is necessary to identify the individual and group ends of organizational members in order to understand how any one dominant coalition's preferences become the strategy of the firm.

Although Karpik's concern was the multinational corporation and his theoretical interests derive from his study of French-based multinationals, his concepts and methodology can be generalized to other types of organizations. One aim of this study is to extend and apply selected concepts from Karpik's works to public sector human service organizations, especially the administration of such agencies.

Logics of Action. Karpik's concept of logics of action (LAs) is central to his discussion on leadership strategy. Logics of action (1972a: 316-19; 1972b: 89-92; 1972c: 26-31; 1978: 47-49) are defined as the observed rationalities of organizational actors, particularly leaders, from the point of view of the outside observer. LAs are also "the principles of action around which individuals and groups organize their attitudes and behavior" (1978: 47). The essential use of this concept is that it enables the external observer to distinguish between the private objectives as organizational leaders define them and the preferences of these same individuals as observed or reconstructed by the researcher. The confusion or identification between intended and observed leaders' strategies is therefore overcome.

Logics of action represent a broad range of social, economic, and political choices from which organizational actors and leaders are assumed by an outside observer to organize their goal-seeking activities. Examples of the range of logics of actions include prestige, technical profitability, power, innovation, production, and adaptive rationalities. For example, some powerful organizational members in a firm may seek to extend their position by adopting a strategy based on the principle of technical logic; others may use innovation as their guiding principle of acting to achieve their ends.

The concept of logics of action is similar to Perrow's notion of "operative goals" (1963), goals that are observed as actually pursued by leaders, as contrasted with official goals, which are not necessarily implemented by individuals. Operative goals are those private ends of a powerful group or individual leaders who have accomplished their goals throughout the organization.

However, Perrow's notion of operative goals, unlike Karpik's concept of LAs, is studied separately from the political process that gives meaning and context to the means and rationalities used by competing groups to achieve their ends. For Karpik, there may be competing logics of action at any point in time among various organizational coalitions. It is only by studying the political struggles among individuals and coalitions internal and external to the organization that a researcher can identify the actual powerful individuals and the means they used to implement their logics of action.

It should be noted that for Karpik, no single LA dominates all activity in a large firm at all times; rather, there are hier-archies of LAs that dominate an organization's activities, depend-ing on the historical conditions and the shifting power balances within the organization.

Karpik emphasized that the concept of logics of action is "an analytical instrument constructed by the observer, designat-ing forms of coherence among objectives: these then are criteria of evaluation which may be used equally well for organizations as for the social units making them up, and which are valid for decisions and procedures as for individual and collective prac-tices" (1972b). The theoretical functions of the logics of action are, according to Karpik, (1) to "establish similarities and differences between actors who may be socially dispersed"; and (2) to "demonstrate the relations that exist between the organization and its members" (1972b).

Karpik's concept of logics of action, then, is really a tool for establishing the underlying principles that guide organiza-tional leaders' actions in implementing policy. As a conceptual tool, these constructs enable the researcher to reconstruct the actual strategies of organizational actors and to compare these to the intended objectives of these same individuals. Moreover, the logics of action that dominate an organization's activities can also be linked to and understood by studying the enacted policy resulting from the implementation of a particular logic of action. This process leads to a wider understanding of the social and historical environment and of other organizational effects on the implementing firm. Reminiscent of Selznick, Karpik called his approach a "socio-historical" perspective for studying organizations. He stated that although the organization "occupies a central position as an empirical reality . . . it is merely a basis upon which to examine the relations between science and economy, between the economy and the other insti-tutions, and between institutions and social relations" (1978: 64).

Three Empirical Examples of the Strategic
Choice Perspective

Although a number of empirical studies exist to support
the theoretical premises presented in this second view of organizational leadership as purposive activity (Allison 1971; Baldridge
1971; Stone 1974; Hirsch 1969; Meyer 1978), the following three
studies (Gallie 1978; Hage and Dewar 1973; Miles 1982) are
briefly illustrated to demonstrate the role of leadership and
societal values leaders adopt as determinants of organizational
change.

Duncan Gallie (1978; see also Zey-Ferrell and Aiken 1981)
conducted a survey of 800 workers in four refineries, two each
in France and Britain. One of his major findings was that the
attitudes of French and British workers toward management
control techniques differed substantially, even though they
worked for the same companies. Also, because of the different
value systems of the French and British workers, management
control strategies that worked with one national group were not
effective with the other. Gallie states,

given the structure of power in the French refineries,
French claims for greater efficiency are not altogether
implausible. Management could draw up a blueprint
for the organizational structure that would maximize
efficiency, and then quite simply impose it by fiat.
British management, in contrast, but adopting a
semi-constitutional strategy, necessarily accepted
powerful constraints on its freedom of action. (1978:
311)

This finding suggests that the effectiveness of leadership
control strategies in organizations depends to a large extent
on the fit between the values held by the employees and the
strategies used.

Hage and Dewar (1973) studied a small number of welfare
agencies in the Midwest to determine whether or not elite values
or organizational structure predicted innovation. Elites were
identified by the formal authority members held in the organizational structure and by the number of decisions in which these
individuals participated. The variable indicating membership
values was measured by a battery that identified the recognition
of need for change in the environment. The structural variables
included indicators of centralization, complexity, and formalization. Innovation was measured by programs that involved new
activities for clients. The indicators of values were measured

in 1964 and those for program innovations in 1967. The findings indicated that measures of leadership values were a stronger predictor of program innovation than were structural variables. The correlations for leadership values and change exceeded 0.60. None of the structural variables, except complexity, approached the strength of this correlation. Moreover, the partial correlations between elite values and innovation when controlling for structure were even higher than 0.60. These authors concluded that the values of the organizational elite are more important than the general organizational membership values in predicting program innovation.

In an intensive case study, Miles (1982) examined the six largest U.S. tobacco companies and their response to threats faced by this industry between 1950 and 1975. Miles addressed the questions: What were the strategic options available to organizations for adapting to external stress? and What was the effectiveness of the implemented strategies in the industry? Miles only secondarily addressed the topic of how and by what means industry leaders chose their strategies.

Miles' study offers an interesting model for examining organizational strategies in response to external changing conditions; however, he failed to explain the tactics the individual industry leaders intended and actually used in enforcing their interests in the marketplace. For example, the reader is never told how the tobacco executives' predispositions or the resulting policy outcomes were related to their interests. In fact, Miles leaves the reader with the impression that the tobacco industry leaders unintentionally failed to achieve their intended public policy objectives. For example, the reader is asked on little evidence to accept Miles' argument that the warning labels that were put on all cigarette packages and which acted as a legal protection from liability litigation, were an unintentional side effect of the industry's strategies. Also, Miles did not explain the tobacco leaders' multinational strategies, or the power they exerted in foreign markets.

While Miles' study has many useful concepts and clues about how to qualitatively examine corporate leaders' strategies, his own work falls short of his research objectives because, we maintain, he used an adaptive, natural selection perspective to analyze corporate political interests. Thus, the question arises: Whose interests were served and whose intentions became policy? This was not answered.

The Two Views in Retrospect

The theoretical dichotomy between the two views presented above does not preclude the relevance of both to this study. In fact, consistent with the first view of organizational leadership is the acknowledgment here that environmental factors are important in affecting leaders' decisions. However, the nature, extent, and impact of environmental influences are viewed here as research questions to be examined. Environmental factors are not considered here as predetermined—rather, these are historically, politically, and economically formed and may be altered by leaders' actions.

Not all executives in organizations are successful in implementing desired strategies. Some policies may certainly evolve by default or in spite of leadership. However, we argue that by adopting a strategic choice perspective to study organizational change and policy implementation, researchers become aware of the role of leaders and the political process—both factors have been neglected in organizational studies over the last decade.

Underlying Assumptions of This Study

The assumptions underlying this study are largely based on the strategic choice perspective presented above. The assumptions include:

1. Organizations may best be conceptualized as political arenas of competing individuals and groups with varying interests. They seek to manipulate internal and external organizational resources to achieve their ends.

2. Top-level executives have the most power and authority to control internal organizational arrangements in order to dominate external factors in obtaining specific ends. It is the initiation of organizational structure to formulate specific implementation strategies that is the major internal organizational activity of top administrators in making policy. The major external organizational activity of a top administrator in making policy is the evaluation of environmental constraints, resources, and groups in determining a viable strategy; the selection of a strategy; and guiding the implementation process of the strategy.

3. The implemented policy outcomes of organizations represent the interaction between the implementing administrator's strategy, environmental factors and groups, and internal organizational politics. By reconstructing the political process in which policy is implemented, the organizational researcher is able to determine the principal individuals responsible for implementing the policy, the intended and the observed strategy of the implementing leader, the administrator's use of organizational structure, and the environmental factors involved.

4. Organizations' histories are embodied in the policies, strategies, and political processes in which administrative leaders

implement their logics of action. In order to understand the formulation and implementation of particular policies, it is therefore necessary to examine this organizational history.

Aim of This Study

This study examines the dominant strategies of three top administrators in what has been a progressive state vocational rehabilitation agency. The period covered in this study spans twenty years (1961-80). The specific policy area focused on here is the state administrators' use of and negotiations with private sheltered facilities to train and place handicapped clients in competitive jobs.

This is an important area of research for the following reasons: first, there are vocational rehabilitation organizations in every state and many abroad. Congress authorizes over $850 million annually to these organizations. These organizations spend varying amounts of funds in private sheltered facilities that were created to assist in the rehabilitation of handicapped clients by providing work as a training medium. The funds a state vocational rehabilitation agency allots to these private facilities also varies. In the past, as much as 50 percent of some state agencies' budgets were expended in sheltered workshops. As an area of policy implementation research, this type of agency represents an interesting topic.

Second, the discretion of a state administrator in a vocational rehabilitation agency in formulating strategy and implementing policy regarding the use of sheltered rehabilitation facilities is often considerable. The ways in which these organizational leaders manipulate legal, political, and fiscal resources to implement policy in this area is a subject for research. Third, although there have been studies that examined the analysis of policy development and promulgation problems in the state/ federal vocational rehabilitation system, no study to date has focused on the individual strategy and policy implementation activities of state administrators, especially regarding the use of private facilities to rehabilitate clients vocationally.

2

Research Strategy

Examining the strategy-making process of administrators requires an action-oriented approach. Such an approach should accommodate a longitudinal dimension, identify alternatives that were available to the policy implementors, and determine the outcomes of the policy choices. A qualitative research approach was used to study administrative strategies in this study. Karpik's logics of action concept is extended to include a goal-attainment framework. Also, parts of Allison's governmental politics model are used to explain process issues in the study. A set of hypotheses was developed to structure our observations. These elements of our research approach are explained below.

LOGICS OF ACTION: GOAL-ATTAINMENT
FRAMEWORK FOR LINKING LEADERS'
STRATEGIES TO POLICY OUTCOMES

Karpik's concept of the logics of action (LAs) is a major part of the research strategy used in this study. The logics of action concept enables the researcher to examine the origin, nature, and transformation of major organizational policy by reconstructing the individual ends and means of powerful leaders and coalitions. Individual objectives and strategies are also reconstructed from observed policy outcomes. This research process is situationally and historically grounded and is retrospective in nature.

Karpik's aim is consistent with that of Weber (1968): namely, Karpik did not intend to predict, but tried to understand and

explain social phenomena from an individual, action perspective.
For Weber and Karpik, purpose, value, and intentionality play
a primary role in individual and collective behavior, especially
as this behavior is conditioned by the larger societal context.
This research tradition provides an alternative to Durkheimian
positivism that explains social reality from a functional, non-
purposive empiricist perspective. The Weberian methodological
tradition has more recently been reflected in European organizational analysts' works, such as those of Karpik and Crozier.

The theoretical basis of the LAs analysis derives from
Karpik's concern for a socio-historical perspective of organizations. Such a perspective maintains that the individual is the
starting point for examining organizational policy. As Cyert
and March (1963) contended, individuals have goals, intentions,
and preferences; organizations do not. Also, organizational
members are conscious problem solvers, not passive instruments
or structural components of organizations. Moreover, actions
of organizational members are grounded in the specific historical,
cultural, and situational dynamics of their organizations. By
examining strategies of organizational leaders, the researcher
also reconstructs the environmental and internal organizational
constraints that enable particular leaders to implement successfully or fail to enact intended policy.

Because individual actors formulate their strategy and act
on the basis of their personal decision-making criteria, it is
necessary for the researcher to reconstruct and identify the
ends and means of the leaders' intentions (see Simon 1976).
The means (strategies) are the intended activities individuals
believe appropriate for achieving their objectives. It is the
task of the researcher to interpret and establish the intended
strategies and objectives of individual actors by identifying
the dominant motives and rationales from their multiple strategy-
making activities.

Since intended strategies and objectives of organizational
leaders may not in fact be realized, however, the researcher is
obliged to identify those implemented policy ends and resultant
strategies that were used. This task involves the attempted
reconstruction of the decision-making process and policy outcomes of individual organizational actors empowered and responsible for implementing policy.

It is, then, through the systematic identification of (1)
the powerful principal actors involved in the entire policymaking
arena, (2) the policy implementing organizational leadership's
intended ends and means, (3) the resultant policy outcome, and
(4) the relationship between the intended (or unintended) strate-

gies and the realized strategies of the implementing organization's leaders, that the process and substance of policymaking activities and the role of organizational leaders in the process can be understood and evaluated.

A Goal-Attainment Framework

Karpik examines organizational goal-attainment activities from two perspectives: the point of view of the organizational members who themselves enact policy, and that of the outside observer or researcher. From the perspective of the organizational actor, the intended or stated ends of goal achievement are identified and distinguished from the view of the researcher. The actors' actual or implemented objectives are also observed separately from the methods the actors use to achieve their desired ends. These two perspectives represent Karpik's concern with distinguishing between intentional and realized ends and means of goal-seeking activities.

Karpik carefully defined objectives, strategy, logics of action, and politics (or policy outcomes) in order to include these dimensions in a single theoretical perspective for examining goal-attainment behavior of organizational members. Karpik's conceptual distinctions among these terms represent one of his major contributions toward resolving the dilemma of how to study individual strategy and relate this to policy outcomes in organizations.

Definitions

Objectives for Karpik are the intentional ends of individual organizational actors or coalitions of actors who collectively agree on shared cognitive ends. They are privately held ends that organizational leaders articulate among their inner circle. These intentional ends may or may not be realized. Objectives can exist essentially as desired future states from the point of view of the actor. They do not represent implemented ends. They are not the official goals of an organization, but are the informal ends of the organization's leader or the dominant coalition. Leaders may not have clearly defined objectives. Identifying the presence or absence of these objectives is the task of the researcher. The question is, Whose objectives are being sought?

Strategies are, according to Karpik, commitments of the allocation of an organization's resources by its leaders. They

are the intentional means and methods of the organization's
leaders for carrying out their objectives. Like objectives,
strategies may or may not be realized. Strategies, therefore,
represent the conscious and deliberate ways leaders seek to
achieve their desired objectives or ends. Strategies are plans
held by organizational leaders or powerful individuals (Chandler
1969). The extent to which these plans for achieving particular
ends are realized is also a research task.

Logics of action are Karpik's central orienting concept.
Karpik defines LAs (1972a:316-19; 1972b:89-92; 1972c:26-31;
1978:47-49) as the observed rationalities of organizational actors
or a dominant coalition from the point of view of the researcher.
LAs are "the principles of action around which individuals and
groups organize their attitudes and behavior" (1978:47). Logics
of action can also be viewed as the realized strategies of organizational leaders.

Logics of action cover a wide range of choice domains:
LA adaptive, LA prestige, LA technical, LA production, LA
profitability, LA power, and LA innovation. Extending beyond
the economic, effectiveness, or performance strategic principles,
this concept enables the researcher to probe into a wide spectrum
of motivational areas that may stimulate leaders to implement
particular choices.

In this study LAs are viewed as implemented strategies.
LAs can, then, be compared to strategies of organizational
leaders, since strategies are considered intentional means of
achieving objectives.

Policy outcomes (what Karpik referred to as politiques)
are the implemented outcomes of objectives. Policy outcomes
are the realized choices of organizational leaders and other
members. What existed as various alternatives for possible
implementation (objectives) when actualized become policy.
These are also established from the point of view of the observer.
Resultant policies may involve a range of actors and actions
limited to the focal organization.

The conceptual scheme in Table 2.1 illustrates Karpik's
four dimensions of goal-attainment activity among organizational
leaders and other powerful actors. Essentially, this illustration
shows goal attainment as conceptualized from (1) the actor's
point of view, that is, from the intended objectives (ends)
and the intended means (strategies) to achieve those objectives;
from (2) the observer's or researcher's point of view—this
illustration shows the implemented policy outcomes and the
realized means (the LAs) of implementing activities.

TABLE 2.1

Goal-Attainment Framework

Point of View	Ends	Means
Actor (intended goal-seeking activities)	Objectives	Strategies
Researcher (implemented goal-seeking activities)	Policy outcomes	Logics of action

Source: Compiled by the author.

The Concept of Game in the Research Strategy

Research questions from Allison's governmental politics model were used to complement Karpik's LAs framework of analysis for this study. The concept of game as elaborated by Allison to study federal bureaucracies has also been used by Bardach (1977) to characterize public policy implementation processes and has been theoretically extended by Crozier and Friedberg (1977) as an instrument to study organizational strategy and collective behavior.

Bardach (1977:56) used the idea of games as a master metaphor "to look at the players, what they regard as the stakes, their strategies and tactics, their resources for playing, the rules of play (which stipulate the conditions for winning), the rules of 'fair' play (which stipulate the boundaries beyond which lie fraud or illegitimacy), the nature of the communications (or lack of them) among the players, and the degree of uncertainty surrounding the possible outcomes."

Crozier and Friedberg (1977:98) view organizations as ensembles of connected games that integrate organizational actors' behavior. They state that organizations are really aggregations of games. The formal and informal rules of games define the spectrum of rational strategies that enable actors to compete to obtain their private ends. They noted that different games have different strategies (1977:102).

They define game as a concrete mechanism used by organizational members to structure and regulate their power relations.

Games impose constraints on actors through rules that are created. Players must abide by these rules in order to win. These authors also note that the roles of individuals in organizations condition their game playing.

The concept of game in organizations as defined and characterized by Bardach, Crozier and Friedberg, and Allison emphasizes the theoretical importance of studying individual organizational members and their strategic activities in implementing policy.

ORIENTING RESEARCH QUESTIONS: ALLISON'S GOVERNMENTAL POLITICS MODEL

Allison's study of the Cuban missile crisis involved the use of an inductive model that is action and process oriented and that is designed to examine individual perspectives on policy issues. He viewed the game played by top-level governmental agency leaders in policy-making decisions as political, involving bargaining over multiple conflicting issues. He also held that governmental decision makers act from several interest bases, such as national, organizational, group, and personal orientations. Objectives deriving from any or all of these are not always actualized; rather, the outcome of a particular policy is a consequence of the pulling and hauling that is politics. Because governmental leaders make decisions within pluralistic but unique situations, Allison developed a set of orienting or guiding questions to explain the results of these decisions. More specifically, he stated, "To explain why a particular formal government decision was made, or why one pattern of governmental behavior emerged, it is necessary to identify the games and players, to display the coalitions, bargains, compromise, and to convey some feel for the confusion."

The following questions are taken from Allison's governmental politics model and are used here to complement Karpik's methodology, which was discussed above. Specifically, these questions are used to determine (1) the powerful actors inside and external to the implementing policy agency who were involved in shaping the outcomes; (2) the positions of the major actors as well as the issues they formulated; (3) the game (parameters of the actors' objectives and influences) in which each set of actors was involved in the policymaking arena; and (4) the decision rules the dominant players created and violated in attempting to implement policy.

1. Who plays? This question enables the researcher to identify the principal individuals and groups inside and external

to the policymaking agency who were influential in the process
of implementing a particular policy. Relevant to this study is
the observation Allison made regarding the positions of players:
"Positions define what players both may and must do. The
advantages and handicaps with which each player can enter
and play in various games stem from his position. So does a
cluster of obligations for the performance of certain tasks"
(1971:164). The limitations and opportunities attached to
positional power must be considered in examining governmental
actors' policymaking influence. Coalitions at the national, state,
and local levels of government and community must also be identified as these players influence policy. For purposes of this
study, groups and coalitions who exert significant influence
on the shaping of policy are identified.

    2. What determines each player's stand? This question,
according to Allison, involves an examination of the power of
the dominant players. Power is a function of "bargaining
advantages, skill and will in using bargaining advantages, and
other players' perceptions of the first two ingredients" (1971:
169). Allison further notes that bargaining capability depends
on (1) formal authority or positional power; (2) control over
resources to enact strategy; (3) information control and expertise
to define resources, choose options, and calculate strategy
enactment possibilities; (4) the ability to influence other
members' objectives in other games; (5) personal persuasive-
ness (defined as charisma, informal relations) with other members; and (6) access and ability to persuade other influential
players in the game.

    3. What is the game? According to Allison, the game is
defined as the players' combined stands, moves, and influences,
which determine the actions and decisions taken. Allison details
how the game is identified by outlining the following dimensions:
(a) action channels, (b) rules of the game, (c) action as political
resultant. Action channels are routine means of effecting action
on specific types of issues. Issues are, in fact, identified within
these channels. Action channels structure the game by pre-
selecting the players, determining their entrance into the game,
and allocating the benefits and disadvantages for each game.
Following Allison's logic, the concept of action channels is
appropriate to large government bureaucracies in which ranking
officials and influential staff are able to make policy within their
official niches and chains of command. For this study, however,
the interaction of nongovernmental coalitions must also be considered in their effect on policymaking activities of administrative
state leaders. The extent to which these coalitions affect the
governmental action channels in the policy implementation process
becomes a research question.

Rules of the game are both implicit and explicit, stable and changing sources of policymaking boundaries. These originate from formal legal sources such as the Constitution, state statutes, and federal laws and regulations. Rules of the game are also found in the culture, such as values and social attitudes. Rules determine the means by which players gain access to action channels, positions of power, and eventually the game of policy implementation. Rules also set boundaries in which government decisions and actions are permitted. For purposes of this study, the rules of the game will be dealt with in two ways. First, the legal aspects of the game will be considered as part of the environmental conditions that constrain or assist administrative leaders in formulating their objectives. Second, rules will be viewed as the internal organizational strategies and the external implementation means by which administrative leaders seek to achieve their own policy objectives.

These questions, then, will complement Karpik's LA framework for analyzing goal-attainment activities by identifying the principal players involved in the policy arena, the dominant issues, and the action channels by which various actors sought to influence policy, and by defining the game (i.e., the arena of issues, stands and objectives) of the actors involved.

GUIDING PRELIMINARY HYPOTHESES

The central theoretical question of this study is Do organizational leaders make a significant difference in affecting policy outcomes? To address this, the following secondary questions must be asked: (1) Under what external legal, economic, and political conditions do administrators adopt certain strategic principles to guide their policymaking activities? The answer must also include the possibility that particular administrators may try to create certain conditions to achieve their goals. (2) What internal organizational arrangements and control prem premises do administrators use during different historical periods to motivate staff as well as external allies to assist them in achieving their goals? What leadership styles are used? (3) What objectives and strategic tactics do administrators use to interpret and implement external environmental conditions to their own policymaking advantage?

Table 2.2 shows a hypothetical set of relationships between organizational leaders' strategic responses to changing environmental conditions. This table is partly based on theory and on assumptions made from literature relating to this topic. The table is explained first, followed by the hypotheses that are based on the table, and which were used to guide the study.

TABLE 2.2

Strategic Leadership Responses to Environmental Factors (Legal, Socioeconomic, Political) during Historical Organizational Changes

Leadership Responses	Growth	Stability*	Critical-turbulence	Cutback
Logic of action Internal control premise	LA expansion Innovation/promotion	LA balance Loyalty	LA productivity Accountability	LA retrenchment Survival
Originating structure	Elaboration/diversification	Centralization	Centralization	Contraction
Style Tactics	Charismatic Stress cooperation	Commander-in-chief Top-down negotiations Personalize mission Routinize tasks Centralize communications	Technically competent Legitimate activities Reaffirm mission Emphasize performance	Politically competent Realign allies Use contingency budgeting Refocus mission
Organizational process(es)	External field operations	Public relations and program research	Measurement, control, and production	Budgeting and political liaison functions

*This period was not observed and therefore not used in this study.

Source: Compiled by the author.

31

Leadership Responses

The dimensions of leadership responses in the typology
are partly derived from organizational theory (e.g., Karpik
1972a, 1972b, 1978; March and Simon 1958) and are an attempt
to depict important roles public agency administrators play in
their policy-implementing activities. The leadership responses
are also an explorative attempt to explain administrative responses
under changing environmental conditions. These responses are
ideal types (Weber 1968) and are not meant to be exhaustive or
exclusive. Rather, they represent responses administrators
could be expected to make to achieve policy goals under certain
historical and environmental conditions.

External Environmental Influences

External environmental influences are grouped under four
general periods: growth, stability, critical-turbulence, and
cutback. External influences include political, socioeconomic,
and legal factors. A stability period was not observed and is
therefore not included in this study.

Political, socioeconomic, and legal influences were selected
as factors comprising external organizational influences because
these represent the most powerful determinants on public administrative policy. The economic influence is defined as the effects
of the national, state, and local economies on the funding level
of the state vocational agency. Since the focus of this study is
on the strategic decisions of state vocational rehabilitation
administrators regarding the funding and use of privately run
sheltered workshops, the socioeconomic sources of workshops'
funding are also a relevant part of this external influence.
Socioeconomic is used instead of the term economic since first,
social values at the national and state government levels affect
funding decisions both for general vocational rehabilitation
programs and for the training of handicapped clients in sheltered
workshops. Second, lobbying efforts also affect the funding
levels of these programs. So funding decisions are rarely just
economic in nature.

The legal influence is defined as the national laws, regulations, and state statutes that are intended to govern the activities of state vocational rehabilitation funding priorities and
policy implementation. Such laws and regulations are also
affected by political activities of individuals and groups involved
in the general field of vocational rehabilitation.

The political influence overlaps the legal and socioeconomic factors but also includes the specific coalition-building activities of groups that attempt to influence state agency administrators' objectives and strategies in the policy area of sheltered rehabilitation facilities.

These three factors, then, compose the external dimensions of the environment. Again, as stated earlier, these influences can be manipulated by state administrators and by other influential actors in this policy area.

Organizational Periods of Change

Environmental factors are grouped into four general periods that represent an overview of the historical influences that the socioeconomic, political, and legal factors have had on vocational rehabilitation agencies in the United States over the last two decades (Wright 1980). These periods do not represent a linear or one-time sequence of influences; rather, these periods depend on agencies' leadership strategies as well as the interaction of other players' actions in this policy area. Also, administrative leaders in vocational rehabilitation agencies across the country do not respond to influences under these external categories in the same way.

The external historical period of growth is characterized by an expanding national economy, which peaked for social services during President Johnson's Great Society era. National values and attitudes toward the socially disadvantaged and the handicapped were supportive of congressional legislation as well as presidential imperatives to fund social services programs. Although state legislation and attitudes varied with the national mood, vocational rehabilitation took 80 percent of its funding from the federal government during this period and continued to do so to the present. Growth as a result of federal and state program funding also involved the possibility of expansion for state and local professional and consumer interest groups in this field.

The period of critical-turbulence refers to times during which state vocational rehabilitation administrators experience legal, political, and/or socioeconomic changes that can threaten their objectives and policy implementation strategies to the point of crisis or administrative succession. This phase is defined and used instead of turbulence because government vocational rehabilitation agency administrators more often than not experience routine or cyclical problems in funding, politics, and legal matters that are characteristic of people-processing agencies. Critical-turbulent phases denote distinct junctures in external conditions that significantly affect administrators' strategic activities.

The period of cutback refers mainly to the socioeconomic climate and funding levels, which usually originate at the national level and extend to the state and local levels of government. As noted by Whetten (1980), research relating to this phase of organizational and administrative activity has been virtually neglected. Until recently, organizational research has been biased with a growth-oriented philosophy (Whetten 1980).

These four periods of historical change in the external environment are used in this study as the context of change that affected and was affected by the VR administrators' strategies.

Leadership responses (Table 2.2) represent the VR state administrative leaders' strategic modes of implementing dominant policy objectives. This dimension is composed of five components: dominant logic of action, internal control premise, style, tactics, and organizational process.

1. The dominant logic of action is based on Karpik's concept (1972b, 1978) and refers to the administrative leader's overall guiding rationale used in implementing his/her strategic choices. This rationale is reconstructed by the observer and conceptually represents the dominant logic(s) the administrator used to implement particular policy objectives.

2. The dominant internal control premise is based on March and Simon's concept (1958). For March and Simon, the premises of decisions and the information flow that supports decision-making activities require control in organizations. Classic bureaucratic controls like division of labor, job classifications, and rules are not sufficient to control decisions made in organizations. Perrow (1979), for example, noted that controls are more important when work is nonroutine and are needed near the top of organizations because "managerial work there is less routine, the consequences of decisions are hard to assess immediately, and access to company resources is greatest" (1979:152).

The literature on definitions and types of controls used in organizations to channel behavior and cognitive premises abounds (e.g., Perrow 1979:150-52; Tannenbaum 1968; Etzioni 1961:233-62; Edwards 1977; Katz and Kahn 1978:302-22, to name a few sources). The concept of dominant internal control premise as used here is based more on March and Simon's notion of premise control and is defined as the particular rationale

developed by the administrator with his/her top-level staff for
the purpose of attempting to convince, persuade, and motivate
staff members at all organizational levels to carry out specific
strategies toward implementing his/her policy objectives. These
controlling premises are consistent with the dominant LAs of
administrators regarding their particular policy objectives.
Such internal control premises are necessary to motivate staff
to comply with responsibilities and communication consistent
with executing policy objectives short of coercive or disciplinary
organizational controls.

   3. The organizational structure as used here refers to
particular arrangements of staff in implementing the organization,
to changing positions and civil service classifications depending
on their assignment authorized by the state agency administrator.
Organizational structure is, in part, a function of the administrator's power to formulate and implement strategy. While there
are legal and organizational constraints intervening between the
administrator's desire and political objective to originate structure (Katz and Kahn 1978) and to meet his/her policy ends, it
is contended here that administrators will apply their formal
and informal influence to the extent necessary to change staffing
patterns they believe advantageous to achieving their ends.

   4. Leadership style. The majority of studies dealing with
leadership style relate to mid- or lower-level management and
attempt to link causally different types of leadership styles to
worker morale and productivity. Proponents of the human
relations school in particular (Likert 1961; McGregor 1960;
Argyris 1962) sought to define leadership styles that emphasized
interpersonal competence. Other studies in this area continued
to focus on leader-follower relationships in the workplace and
dichotomized the relations into two basic dimensions: task direction and socio-emotional supportiveness (e.g., Fiedler 1966).

   More recent studies have attempted to define leadership
philosophies and profiles in terms of matching top management
styles with the organization's context and performance indicators
(Khandwalla 1976; Jauch and Osborn 1981). Katz and Kahn
(1978), however, define leadership style from a systemic
perspective. This involves the top-level administrative leaders'
perception and understanding of external environmental demands
in order to forecast "the probable effects of different courses
of action and consequent choosing among them" (1978:540).
The leader's style involves the "intellective aspect of leadership,"
that is, the individual's "ability to see, conceptualize, appraise,
predict and understand the demands and opportunities posed
to the organization by its environment" (1978:540). Katz and

Kahn have discussed only one leadership style from this perspective, that of charisma. This study extends their concept to include other styles that are assumed to be appropriate with changing contexts. The assumption here is that leaders will adopt styles that enable them to respond to changing demands in order to successfully implement their policy objectives.

5. Tactics is a concept that has not been conceptually distinguished by some researchers from strategy. Others, however, have skillfully written on tactics (e.g., Wildavsky 1968) but have not linked these to strategy. Here tactics is defined as specific maneuvers administrators use to manipulate internal and external organizational sources in order to achieve their broader strategic policy objectives.

Taken together, these elements of administrators' strategic responses represent consistent modes for implementing policy objectives. Based on definitions and terms illustrated and explained in Table 2.2, we present the hypotheses used to guide the inquiry.

The Hypotheses Explained

The first set of hypotheses relates leadership responses to environmental conditions during a period of historical growth.

H-1. Administrative leaders who can successfully select and implement expansionist objectives and strategies in an external environment characterized by growth increase the likelihood of creating bureaucratic domains and empires.

H-1a. A leadership style that is charismatic during growth periods enables administrators to select and successfully implement expansionist objectives and strategies.

H-1b. Use of major external negotiation tactics of cooperation and alliance building enables administrators to successfully select and implement strategies to enlarge their domain within a growth environment.

H-1c. Administrators who originate or change their organizational structures by elaborating the organization and diversifying operational arrangements increase the likelihood of successfully implementing expansionist strategies within a growth environment.

H-1d. The dominant organization processes administrators will use to increase their domains in growth environments are field-related operations combined with planning.

H-1e. Administrators who, during growth periods, select and implement a dominant internal control strategy of innovation, increase the likelihood of motivating their staff to implement expansionist objectives and strategies.

The second set of hypotheses relates leadership strategic responses to environmental conditions during a critical-turbulence phase.

H-2. Administrative leaders who can successfully select and implement production-related objectives and strategies in an external environment characterized by critical turbulence increase the likelihood of protecting their desired organizational domain.

H-2a. A leadership style that is technically competent during critically turbulent periods will enable administrators to select and successfully implement and emphasize production objectives and strategies.

H-2b. Major external negotiation tactics of legitimating and emphasizing productivity will increase the likelihood of administrators' protecting their desired organizational domain during critically turbulent periods.

H-2c. Administrators who originate or change their organizational structures by centralizing decision making increase the likelihood of implementing production objectives and strategies during a critically turbulent period.

H-2d. The dominant organizational process administrators will use to increase the likelihood of protecting their domain is evaluation and control.

H-2e. Administrators who, during critically turbulent periods, select and implement a dominant internal control strategy of accountability increase the likelihood of motivating their staff to implement production-related strategies.

Finally, during periods of cutback administrators are faced with problems that many have not experienced in their careers, at least in the magnitude and immediacy the Reagan administration policies have posed for social service sector leaders. Therefore,

H-3. Administrative leaders who can successfully select and implement retrenchment objectives and strategies within environments characterized as cutback increase the likelihood of maintaining organizational autonomy and survival.

H-3a. A leadership style that is characterized as politically competent during cutback periods enables administrators to select and implement retrenchment objectives and strategies more successfully.

H-3b. Adoption of major external negotiation tactics of realigning allies and resources and refocusing mission, enhance the likelihood of administrators' successfully implementing retrenchment objectives and strategies within cutback environments.

H-3c. Administrators who originate or change their organizational structures by contracting size and combining functions enhance their likelihood of successfully implementing retrenchment objectives and strategies within environments characterized by declining resources.

H-3d. The dominant organizational processes administrators will use to increase their opportunities to retrench are budgeting and political liaison activities.

H-3e. Administrators who, during environments characterized as cutback, select and implement a dominant internal control strategy of survival increase the likelihood of motivating their staff to implement retrenchment strategies.

The hypotheses are preliminary generalizations that are revised with the reconstruction of observed events in the study.

RESEARCH SCHEME

The conceptual methodologies of Karpik, Allison, and the hypotheses identified earlier serve as the guiding framework for reconstructing the linkages among administrative strategies, environmental forces, and resultant policy outcomes. This study included the time periods and activities occurring within the three principal administrators' terms in office. The rationale for this organization was based on the focus of this study: the examination of the strategic policy responses of the three administrators during changing historical and environmental periods. The names of all individuals and organizations in this study have been changed. All dates and established facts, however, are actual. The following chapters present the temporal boundaries of the study: Chapter 4, strategies during the growth period, 1961-74; Chapter 5, strategies during the critically turbulent years, 1975-78; Chapter 6, retrenchment strategies during the cutback years, 1979-81. Chapter 3 provides the federal historical context and explains the vocational rehabilitation system.

Use of Critical Incidents

A major research method used to identify the goal-attainment activities and policies during each administrator's term was that

of the "critical incident" (Flanagan 1958, 1954; Kay 1959; Mintzberg 1973). The critical incident method involves the collection
of information on a series of important or critical events through
a variety of research techniques, including interviews, studying
records, and questionnaires. The results of these incidents
are examined by the researcher to determine their significance
in the basic inquiry. This method was used by Mintzberg to
study managers' behavior in the workplace. Mintzberg (1973:
223) noted that, "The critical incident technique is interesting
and useful because it focuses on concrete examples, allowing
the manager to describe what he knows best (actual events),
and leaving interpretation of data and development of theory
to the researcher. Its main disadvantage is that one can never
be sure that important parts of the job are not missing from the
description."

Limitations and Advantages of the Research Approach

The major advantages of the research scheme included:
first, studying policy formation activities of top-level administrators required access and methods that enabled us to observe
and record the intentionality, power, and bargaining processes
of individuals and groups (Allison 1971; Benson 1977). The
qualitative concept and methods described above met these
requirements. Second, according to Kimberly (1976:322-30),
five advantages of longitudinal research as exemplified in the
design of this study include: (a) Facilitating attempts to establish
causality. Cross-sectional data limit attempts to establish
causality because of the snapshot nature of the information.
In longitudinal research, temporal precedence can be established
at least within the constraints of available data (1976:325).
(b) Longitudinal research helps to minimize the problem of
inferring process from cross-sectional data. In this study
the process as well as policy outcomes are the focus of the
study. (c) Longitudinal research facilitates the development
of better models of organizational growth and change. (d)
Longitudinal research permits the inclusion of contextual constraints in the research design. Kimberly notes (1976:328),
"It is often argued that longitudinal research can enhance
the substantive significance of research outcomes by permitting
the investigator to gain sufficient familiarity with the setting
that modifications of either instruments or design can be made
where appropriate to reflect important dimensions of the setting."
(e) Longitudinal research enhances the effectiveness of intervention strategies for organizational change. Because this type
of research attempts to sort out causality, provides understand-

ing of process in the organizational events studied, and identifies contextual constraints, it can, according to Kimberly, aid in the design of more effective intervention strategies. Third, multiple research methods as used in this study enable the researcher to examine a variety of organizational processes and levels of organizational activity. Policymaking activities require more than one research method to understand adequately and reconstruct the process as well as the results of the policy domain under consideration (Hambrick and Snow 1980:537).

Limitations

Certain limitations in the research design of this study include the following. First, although this study included the universe of private sheltered rehabilitation facilities used and funded by a particular state vocational rehabilitation agency, and involved within- and across-case examination of the relationships among the network of organizations and individuals involved in the state agency's use of these facilities, still the question persists of whether to generalize the results from a single case study in this area.

Second, the questions of reliability and validity of results also arise when nonstatistical techniques are used, especially in studies that rely on individual perceptions and participant observation. Reliability has been defined as "the extent to which a given measure is stable and yields reproducible results" (Kimberly 1976:338). Validity, the soundness of truth of the results of the study, has also been considered by psychometricians as a function of the reliability of the measures used in a study. However, Kimberly has argued (1976) that issues of reliability and validity have been the predominant concern of psychometricians in dealing with studies limited to problems and issues in organizations. Kimberly continues by stating that research on organizations raises problems of reliability, but of a different nature. Most variables used in studies on organizations are aggregated. Individuals in such studies move around and affect organizational structures and variables under study. Kimberly notes that in the case of any particular organization new individuals entering and leaving an organization may change the results of an aggregated variable between measurement interventions. This change may not be detected even by the most reliable statistical techniques. Longitudinal and qualitative research techniques can incorporate such changes in the study; however, when considering the question of reliability in measuring perceptions of organizational individuals, a quote by Kimberly (1976:340) is worth noting here:

"I would argue that on questions requiring perceptions, the extent of homogeneity in perceptions by different individuals of the same stimulus is not a measure of reliability as some might contend, with close agreement taken as an indicator of high reliability, but rather is a measure of consensus or lack thereof about various aspects of the organization and may itself be used as an important predictor of various outcomes."

3

Historical Overview: The Public Vocational Rehabilitation System and Private, Sheltered Training Workshops

To understand the political games VR administrators and community workshop directors engage in to obtain competitive funding and political turf, it is necessary to understand the larger legislative system in perspective. The underlying economic, political, and social struggles that continue to characterize so many of the relationships between state bureaucrats and community workshop directors stem from this somewhat common historical background. Managing change for state vocational rehabilitation has meant dealing with the demands of workshop directors. We present this background first and then discuss the controversial areas between these focal groups.

PUBLIC VOCATIONAL REHABILITATION:
DEFINITION, HISTORICAL PROGRAM
MISSION AND LEGISLATIVE MANDATES

George Wright defines rehabilitation the following way:

Rehabilitation is a facilitative process enabling a person with a handicap to attain usefulness and satisfaction in life. The individual's handicap may result from any type of disablement (i.e., physical, mental, or emotional) and from various causes (birth defects, sickness and disease, industrial and road accidents, or the stress of war, work and daily life). People are likewise handicapped by cultural disadvantage. . . . Whenever any of

these conditions cause difficulties in life adjustment,
the person is handicapped. Rehabilitation then
equalized opportunity for life attainments as a
human right and societal obligation. (1980:3)

Obermann (1965:345) emphasized the distinguishing characteristic of the vocational rehabilitation program that has, in large
part, ensured its historical survival and separated its main
mission from other welfare and social service programs:

The normal objective in a program of vocational rehabilitation is employment of the client. There is
no easy formula or technique that can be applied to
insure that each rehabilitation client will find work
when he is ready for it. It is usually accepted by
rehabilitation workers that they have not completed
their service to a disabled person until he is securely
placed in a suitable employment and has made the
adjustments necessary to make it reasonably sure
that he will be able to continue that employment.

Vocational rehabilitation, as a public system of services
available to civilians, has evolved from 1917 to 1982 through
over 15 federal legislative acts and amendments. These laws
have progressively added to the definition of clients eligible
for services as well as the expenditures and structure of state
agencies empowered to provide these services. The success
in achieving the passing of these federal laws is attributable
to national and state leaders' lobbying efforts and influence.
State agency directors of vocational rehabilitation programs
have served as one of the foremost lobbying groups on which
national leaders have relied to enact supporting federal
legislation. The following legislative summary highlights the
essential features of the development of the national vocational
rehabilitation program, which helps explain the arena in which
state administrators have worked.

Federal Legislation on Public Vocational
Rehabilitation: 1917-82

Public vocational rehabilitation had its federal legislative
beginning in 1917, at which time Congress initiated the first
Federal Board for Vocational Education. This Board administered
federal funds for vocational rehabilitation programs which were

authorized under the 1918 Smith-Sears Act. In 1920, under
the Smith-Fess Act, civilians were included among the disabled
to receive services. These acts, however, limited the definition
of "disabled" to physical defects or infirmity.

By 1923, 36 states participated in the state-federal program.
The total expenditures in that same year in all the states for
the program were $1,188,081; eight years later the states had
spent only $2 million on this program. By 1923 over one-half
of the funds authorized by the federal government for the states
to operate the program was provided by the states.

Throughout the decade of the 1920s, the conservative
administrations of presidents Harding, Coolidge, and Hoover
were restrictive regarding social welfare expenditures. This
fact combined with that of the administrative structure of the
vocational rehabilitation program being placed under the Federal
Vocation Educational Board did not provide the program with
great fiscal or administrative momentum in its beginnings.

In fact, the disinterest and unfamiliarity of the Federal
Board for Vocational Education with vocational rehabilitational
programs caused tensions between administrators and staff of
these two domains. Moreover, little support was evidenced
from the federal board administering the rehabilitation program
to support national legislation in this area, especially in this
state.

The differences experienced between members of the vocational education system and vocational rehabilitation programs
were basically philosophical. They are worth noting since they
affected the administration of the program at the state level.
Vocational rehabilitation staff emphasized an individualized
approach to assessing clients before providing or purchasing
services leading to rehabilitation. Vocational education staff,
on the other hand, emphasized training as a routine measure.
Vocational rehabilitation staff also stressed that providing
services to the disabled involved interprofessional contacts
and arrangements in the community. These staff members saw
their mission as advocates for rights of handicapped persons
attempting to enter the job market. Vocational educational
professionals were accustomed to more structured, institutionalized, and routine training courses for the disabled. The disabled
were channeled into vocational classes and schools, and were
trained for jobs in the marketplace.

In 1920 a Civilian Vocational Rehabilitation Division with a
director was instituted as part of the Federal Vocational Educational Board in Washington, D.C. The administrative authority
for operating the program was with the Federal Educational Board.

As Obermann (1965:254) noted, vocational rehabilitation programs were placed under different state governing bodies.
In the early years of the program, vocational educational boards
often ran these programs.

From the inception of the state-federal vocational rehabilitation program, congressional commitment and funding were
temporary. Continuing opposition to the program focused on
the constitutional issue of whether the federal government was
funding a program that belonged to the states (Wright 1980).
The program continued to survive from year to year. Forty-
four states participated by 1930, and between 1921 and 1930
over 45,000 persons had received rehabilitation services at a
federal expense of $12 million.

The Great Depression and Vocational
Rehabilitation Legislation

With the Great Depression and President Roosevelt's comprehensive economic recovery and welfare programs, vocational
rehabilitation programs managed to survive. By 1933, Roosevelt
transferred the Federal Board for Vocational Education to the
Department of the Interior. The Commissioner of Education
was responsible for what then became the Federal Rehabilitation
Service. As a consequence, vocational rehabilitation had gained
some administrative independence at the federal level.

In 1935, and for the first time since its inception, permanent
authorization for annual vocational rehabilitation grants to states
was congressionally passed under the Social Security Act. Along
with $1,938,000 annually committed was $102,000 a year for the
administration of the program. Then in 1939 amendments to this
act committed $3.5 million for annual state grants to the program.
Without the lobbying efforts of the National Rehabilitation Association, which was and is composed of rehabilitation professionals
and consumers at national and state levels, however, vocational
rehabilitation provisions in the 1935 act would not have materialized (Wright 1980:138).

From 1920 to 1943, the federal administrative agency
responsible for overseeing the vocational rehabilitation changed
three times. These agencies included the Federal Board for
Vocational Education and the Department of the Interior and,
in 1943, the Office of Vocational Rehabilitation was created.
Noteworthy, however, is the fact that the federal rehabilitation
director remained in that position from 1921 to 1943. The stability
of that position aided in the building of the political coalition

and support of legislation which kept the program viable and
visible at the federal level.

In 1943, the Barden-LaFollette Act expanded the scope of
the program significantly: clientele eligibility now included the
emotionally disturbed and the mentally retarded as well as the
physically disabled; services could be provided to clients that
heretofore were not allowed (e.g., any services necessary to
render a disabled individual fit to engage in a remunerative
occupation were included in the legislation).

In 1951, Mary E. Switzer was appointed Federal Director,
Office of Vocational Rehabilitation, and served until 1970. It
was under her leadership that state vocational rehabilitation
administrators gained substantial access to the federal legislative
process and were able to give their direct support to this policy
arena. Wright (1980) contends it was her influence, together
with the support of national and state vocational rehabilitation
organizations, that enabled the program not only to survive
but to grow during the Eisenhower administration. Under her
influence the 1954 Hill-Burton Act was passed. This act enlarged
the amount of funding to states for the program and provided
for the establishment, alteration, or expansion of rehabilitation
facilities and workshops. These workshops trained lower-level
clients who could not be accepted in vocational technical schools.
This legislation also provided the funding that marked a beginning
in the building and maintenance of sheltered rehabilitation facilities, which are of major interest in our study.

The Great Growth Phase of Vocational
Rehabilitation Legislation

From 1954 to 1964, vocational rehabilitation expenditures
increased from $23 million to $125 million. The "great growth
period," as termed by Wright (1980), was just beginning. Under
the Johnson administration federal legislation was expanded
beyond all previous fiscal and programmatic boundaries. The
1965 Vocational Rehabilitation Act substantially increased funding
for the building and maintenance of sheltered facilities to train
clients. The act also increased research and innovative projects
relating to the program. Most significantly, this act accelerated
the growth of the program by allotting 75 percent funds to state
agencies (Wright 1980:157). The remainder (25 percent) had
to be matched at the state level. Now statewide planning for
program expansion and for developing sheltered facilities could
be realized. This legislation also permitted the state educational

agency or an agency of two or more organizational units that administered one or more public education, health, welfare, or state labor programs to administer the vocational rehabilitation program. For the first time, states were legislatively capable of separating vocational rehabilitation programs from state vocational educational boards. This was a giant step forward philosophically and operationally for state and local VR programs. Autonomy was within reach.

In 1967 further legislative amendments increased the federal allotments for the rehabilitation program to $500 million for 1969 and $600 million earmarked in 1970. Also in 1967, the HEW secretary together with Mary Switzer reorganized the vocational rehabilitation agency into an expanded umbrella agency that was to house the full range of social service programs of Johnson's Great Society. The agency was called the SRS (Social and Rehabilitation Services). Mary Switzer was appointed the first director and reported directly to the Health, Education and Welfare Secretary. Never before or since has the vocational rehabilitation administrative apparatus been as large, powerful, or as visible at the federal level.

Funding for the vocational rehabilitation program alone was authorized at $700 million in 1971. Also in the Vocational Rehabilitation Amendments of 1968, the federal share of the program was increased to 80 percent with the states having to match only 20 percent of those funds. Money was also provided for the creation and development of the rehabilitation facilities beyond the former levels authorized.

The operational challenge would come at the state level, where legislation had to be interpreted and implemented by state vocational rehabilitation administrators.

The increased scope and range of clients federally legislated to enter vocational rehabilitation programs continued. Under the Developmental Disabilities and Facilities Construction Act of 1970, facilities were built to accommodate mentally retarded clients who also became part of the vocational rehabilitation's domain and responsibility. The developmentally disabled included clients with epilepsy, cerebral palsy, and a neurological condition related to mental retardation.

In effect, vocational rehabilitation had become an institution and model social service delivery system during this period, a system that was applied to a wide range of disabilities.

Also, because of the deinstitutionalization movement in many states, individuals with a wide range of disabilities who had been warehoused in correctional and mental institutions for treatment and/or containment, now could become eligible

to enter community rehabilitation programs for training. The
vocational rehabilitation system became the front door of these
facilities; eligible clients assessed as feasible for obtaining
competitive employment with adequate training were also referred
in large numbers to sheltered workshops from vocational rehabilitation programs. During this growth phase, all service providers
gained access to federal grants.

The Battle Phase of Vocational Rehabilitation Legislation

Following the program's unprecedented growth period under
the Johnson administration, 1970 became the battle phase for
vocational rehabilitation. The Nixon era had begun. Coupled
with a conservative administration at the national level was the
loss of leadership for the federal program—Mary Switzer retired
in 1970. Nixon's administration moved to dismantle the leadership of the Social and Rehabilitation Service Agency, which had
been under Switzer's direction. Now a smaller federal organization would oversee the program; the RSA (Regional Service
Administration) was created. Nixon's administration also deemphasized the vocational rehabilitation approach to serving
welfare and correctional populations. A law enforcement emphasis
was applied to the correctional area instead of rehabilitation,
and the welfare population was encouraged to return to the
labor force.

Nixon's approach, however, was not entirely successful.
While he managed to effectively decrease the domain of vocational
rehabilitation in the service areas of corrections and welfare,
he was not able to shrink significantly the basic funding of the
program. Between 1970 and 1973 several presidential vetoes
and congressional veto overrides occurred before the 1973
Rehabilitational Act finally became law: severely disabled clients
were given priority for services (although the terms severely
disabled or severely handicapped were never operationally
defined in the legislation). During 1974, $650 million, and in
1975, $680 million was authorized for the program.

Sheltered, nonprofit community workshops continued to
expand their influence and role in federal legislation. For
example, up to 100 percent mortgage insurance was authorized
to cover their construction costs. Clients' rights were also
expanded. This legislation mandated that vocational rehabilitation counselors develop and jointly agree on individual rehabilitation plans of service with each client. Affirmative action and
nondiscrimination statements were written into the legislation.

State administrators again faced a situation of having to interpret and implement new and somewhat vague legal directives
at the local level, and in an expanded arena that included
different service providers.

The Ford Administration

President Ford's attempted vetoes to curtail the vocational
rehabilitation program were not successful against a Democratic
Congress that gained importance after the Watergate events.
The Rehabilitation Extension Act of 1976 left intact the legislation
of 1973. In fact, funds to the state-federal program increased
from $680 million to $720.3 million per year during this time.
Even without the independence it had under the Johnson administration, the federal agency maintained its visibility and
funding strength at the national level.

The Carter Administration

Under President Carter the vocational rehabilitation program rebounded. The 1978 amendments to the Rehabilitation
Act of 1973 extended the rehabilitation legislation for four years.
Over $1 billion was authorized for 1979. This legislation was
a mandate to serve individuals so severely disabled that they
did not have the potential for remunerative employment. Enabling
clients to live independently became a programmatic mandate
for vocational rehabilitation.

Significant administratively also was Carter's creation of
the Department of Education (DOE). To administer the vocational
rehabilitation program, the Office of Special Education Rehabilitation Services was created and housed with the DOE. Since the
DOE was a relatively small organization, the rehabilitation part
of it would receive more visibility than it did under Ford's
Office of Human Development. Wright (1980:156) noted,

> Perhaps the attractiveness of the remarriage with
> education was a reaction to the recent domination
> of rehabilitation by welfare in the HEW Social and
> Rehabilitation Service Administration and the current
> trend in Florida and other states for a general human
> service agency combining rehabilitation and welfare.

The program remains in the Department of Education at
present.

The Reagan Administration

When President Reagan was elected in 1980, he introduced his new federalism policy, which represented a major shift in the philosophy and funding of health, welfare, educational, and rehabilitation services. Underlying this policy was his expressed intent to return federally legislated entitlement programs to the states. Such a policy was seemingly consistent with Reagan's campaign promise to lessen government's role in the lives of people. His policy promised to consolidate distinct health and social service programs into block grants. The federal government would continue funding these block programs at a greatly reduced amount (from 25 to 65 percent reductions over the three-year period 1982 through 1984). However, state governments would also be expected to assist in the funding and would entirely administer the programs.

Vocational rehabilitation was one program to be included in the Reagan administration's block grant plan. According to the block grant plan, if it were implemented, over sixty years of federal legislation in vocational rehabilitation would be diminished.

As of the spring of 1982, Congress had exempted the vocational rehabilitation program from becoming part of the block grant concept. Moreover, the Reagan administration's proposed appropriation of $767 million for the program in 1982 was met by successful opposition in Congress. A compromise of $863 million was authorized and appropriated until March 1982.

The vocational rehabilitation program, like all human service programs, has operated and continues to function in a highly uncertain federal legislative and fiscal environment. State budgets for social and rehabilitation services have been as tenuous as federal budgets. Under President Reagan's proposed block grant program, however, the threat to most human service programs went beyond the question of funding adjustments and challenged the very existence and mission of such programs. While the vocational rehabilitation program had a stronger national and state network, state VR agency directors had begun to strategize about the effects new federalism policy would have on their services. At the time of this writing the VR program federal funding has remained stable.

Concluding Comments

The summary presented above illustrates a history of over sixty years of federally legislated vocational rehabilitation pro-

grams. The creation and development of the public VR system
began and remains essentially a state-federal program. While
congressional laws originated and currently sustain the program
with 80 percent funding, it is still the state governmental VR
agencies that interpret, implement, and justify this system.
Also, it was and is the state vocational rehabilitation administrators who individually and collectively in their professional
organizations support the federal administrative part of the
program by demonstrating the utility and success of the program
at the local level.

The next section of this chapter explains the organizational
network of VR services with emphasis on the state agency's
role in this system. Because of the centrality of the state
agency's place in the VR system, both programmatically and
politically, and because the specific leadership activities of
state agency administrators have not been systematically
examined—especially in relationship to a particular policy area
over time—the following discussion is designed to explain the
state-federal vocational rehabilitation system, with emphasis
on the role of state agencies.

THE PUBLIC VOCATIONAL REHABILITATION SYSTEM:
THE NATIONAL, STATE, AND LOCAL NETWORKS

The public vocational rehabilitation program is a decentral-
ized administrative and service delivery system that operates
at the federal, regional, and state levels of government.

A description of the operating responsibility of the VR
system in general is quoted by Gellman (1973):

> Federal and state funds are dispersed through
> the state rehabilitation agencies, which provide
> direct services for clients and purchase or pro-
> cure from other public or private agencies such
> services as are not provided by the state agency.
> The typical state agency assesses applicant eligi-
> bility; accepts clients for rehabilitation services;
> evaluates rehabilitants for rehabilitation potential
> . . . and provides counseling, training or further
> education, and job placement either directly or
> indirectly. State agencies refer rehabilitants to
> and purchase services from medical institutions
> and physicians, rehabilitation centers, workshops,
> and educational facilities. The costs are met (in
> part) by the government.

It can be seen from this description that the state VR agency is pivotal in the system since it is at this level that services are actually provided. However, Gellman's description does not explain the role of the federal and regional levels of the system, especially as these relate to the state level.

The Federal Level

The federal level of the program, called since 1967 the Rehabilitation Services Administration (RSA), currently operates within the Department of Education. The commissioner and staff at this level are responsible for the formalization of VR policy as derived from federal legislation. Members at this level succeed in researching and publishing procedures that attempt to assist states in operationalizing congressional legislation. However, the planning and research activities of this section are greatly constrained by (1) overriding priorities and demands congressional leaders place on the agency in their quest to enact particular bills in this area; (2) the cyclical nature of the legislative process that often contradicts continuity of planning efforts; (3) reorganizations of the administering federal agency that houses the program; (4) the competing demands and activities of other federal bureaucracies for political turf, national recognition, visibility, and funding. In the past, RSA officials have attempted to construct a five-year plan to guide their activities and create stability in their policy formation activities. This idea failed because of the constraining factors on the agency listed above. As one evaluative report on the agency noted in 1978, "RSA does its planning through the budgetary process rather than having the budget grow out of an independent long-range plan" (JWK International Corporation 1978:20). One RSA official is quoted in that report as saying, "RSA doesn't have zero-based budgeting; it has zero-based planning."
Given these limitations, the federal level of the system is important in that it assists the enactment of congressional legislation by providing supporting information from state VR agencies; it disperses federal funds to authorized state agencies; it sponsors training and research projects for staff in the system; and it does publish guidelines that assist, even to a limited extent, state administrators and planners in interpreting national laws in the field.

The Regional Level

The regional level of the VR program is an extension of the federal RSA central office. Ten regional commissioners and staff are located nationwide to assist the federal commissioner in ensuring effective promulgation and monitoring of federal policy. These commissioners report directly to the national commissioner. The regional offices have been termed the "eyes and ears" of RSA (the federal level) in the field. Staff from these offices perform program audits and checks of state agency programs. The relationship of regional offices to state agencies is generally cooperative and consultative.

Results of the 1978 study cited above show that the regional offices and RSA are severely limited in their intended activities of operationalizing and monitoring federal legislation to the state VR agencies. Conclusions from this study continue to substantiate the actual operations of the VR system. A major conclusion from the study illustrates the limitations of both the federal and regional levels' mandated tasks.

> The purpose of RSA's policy guidelines is clear neither to RSA nor to the states. Time and again, state agency staff remarked that they use VR legislation and regulations as the prime source for their own directives, not the manual. RSA policy is inconsistently disseminated through regulations, informational memoranda, program instructions, program regulation guides and policy interpretations. This system is disjointed and sorely requires a formal document to provide users some understanding of the order of precedence for these policy vehicles. For the moment, there are two different and discordant kinds of policy within the state/federal VR community: formal RSA policy, which strives to keep up with changing conditions but never quite manages to do so; and the informal policy system within which VR clients live their lives, caseworkers make their daily decisions, and State Directors try to deal with the Feds. The costs of vagueness and obscurity have not been measured, but they must be considerable, judging by the time spent by State and Regional Directors in trying to find out what DHEW and the Congress want them to do (JWK International Corporation, 1978:52).

One of the most serious limitations of the federal and regional levels of the program is the lack of authority each has to impose or enforce sanctions on field operations that violate or fail to properly implement federal policy. As long as state agency administrators attempt to follow the general federal legislation, their federal funding status seems secure. In this sense, state agencies have a wide range of independence vis-à-vis the federal and regional system to implement VR policy.

The State Level

The state governmental level of the public VR system (and the level of particular interest in this study) consists of over 80 agencies, which include those serving only the blind disabled population. The major federal requirement pertaining to the organization of state VR agencies is that each state must have an identifiable unit or division serving the handicapped. Over the last decade, increasing numbers of state VR agencies have become centralized within state umbrella structures, also termed "super-agencies." State governmental umbrella structures include such agencies as Departments of Education, Human Services, and Health and Social Services, which administer several organizational divisions, of which the VR program is a part. Federal level VR administrators and certain congressional representatives have expressed concern about the constraining influence of these umbrella-type structures on the line authority and independence of state VR administrators in implementing VR policy. These umbrella structures tend to impose very centralized bureaucratic rules and overhead costs on VR agencies; these burdens can cut into the service delivery capability of the VR program. VR administrators who choose to merge with such umbrella agencies in the state have done so for any one of several possible reasons: increased personal income and visibility; sharing information and resources with other state-wide programs; proximity to the legislative process; increased capacity to form political allies. Many present-day VR administrators do not favor the status of their agencies operating within large umbrella structures. Decisions to merge with such agencies were made under different historical circumstances than exist now.

Constraints on State VR Administration

Within the state governance system, VR state agency administrators are particularly subject to and constrained by legislators' demands and interests. While state legislatures provide up to 20 percent or more of a VR program's matching federal funds, these governing bodies are subject to competing constituencies, some of which oppose the funding decisions and programmatic strategies of particular VR administrators. Coalitional activity among legislative committees which are pressured by outside groups can directly affect VR funding decisions; this occurred in the state reviewed here.

Another constraining influence on VR administrators is their task of aligning their own administrative line and direct service field staff with specific strategies and objectives. Career trained, educated, and experienced VR personnel tend to coalesce with client-oriented interests rather than with administrators' politically and economically based strategies that are not specifically client related. Value differences between VR line and staff must be considered in examining strategic policy implementation activities.

Given these constraints, VR administrators who are politically skilled and programmatically experienced can chart a course of strategic program activities because of the ambiguity and loopholes in federal and state legislation, and because of the lack of enforcement capability of federal and state governing bodies. To what extent and under what conditions this assertion holds is an empirical question of central interest in this study.

Concluding Comments

The point to be made here about the nature of the state VR agency is the following: it is an organization that operates within a political network of federal and state governmental agencies that often have competing demands supported by varying interests. When these demands are not effectively coordinated or politically executed by powerful interest groups, VR administrators have considerable discretion in interpreting, implementing, and developing program policy at the local and state levels. As important, VR administrators as organizational leaders must also motivate and coordinate their own staffs to accept and implement policies of the administrator's choice.

Within this complex and uncertain programmatic and political environment, VR administrators have a capacity to create and shape policy at the local level to their own career interests and political advantage. In fact, to understand VR policy at the state and local level, it is necessary to reconstruct the demands, constraints, the intended and implemented objectives, and the payoffs that VR administrators orchestrate to maintain their own credibility and mobility. This reconstruction is the focus of this study.

The final section of this chapter explains the major policy area of concern here, to which many VR administrators have devoted the greatest parts of their operating budgets. This area is the funding and use of private rehabilitation facilities, or "workshops," as they are also termed.

The funding of sheltered workshops has been a large part of the state VR administrator's programmatic priorities. Administrators nationwide have allocated between 15 and 60 percent of their program budgets for workshop services in order to obtain these services. Also, workshops and state VR administrators have traditionally viewed their missions as vital to helping the disabled. Economics and program priorities have been important areas shared between these two parties.

This study considers the major strategies of the administrators' entire VR program directions, with specific focus and emphasis on the finding of sheltered workshops. A description and brief historical outline of rehabilitation workshops will facilitate an understanding of the role their leaders have played in the VR program in the specific state under study.

SHELTERED REHABILITATION TRAINING FACILITIES: MISSION, ROLE, AND RELATIONSHIP TO THE VOCATIONAL REHABILITATION SERVICE SYSTEM

Definition of Sheltered Workshops

While there are many types of specialized rehabilitation facilities, this study focuses on the most general of these, which has been defined as a "work-oriented rehabilitation facility with a controlled working environment and individualized vocational goals which utilize work experience and related service for assisting the handicapped person to progress toward normal living and productive vocational status" (sheltered workshops, 1966). Another definition provided by the Federal Fair Labor Standards Act (as quoted in Greenleigh 1975) states that a workshop is a charitable organization or institution conducted not for profit, but for the purpose of carrying out a recognized program of rehabilitation for handicapped workers, and/or for providing such individuals with remunerative employment and other occupational rehabilitating activity of an educational or therapeutic nature.

Sheltered workshops serve a wide range of disabilities. The types of clients served are related to the requirements of funding agencies. Facilities generally offer the following

types of programs for disabled clients: (1) assessment and
evaluation of work potential of clients; (2) work readiness and
vocational exploration programs; (3) work adjustment programs,
in which clients can actually work on assembly-line tasks set
up inside the facility; (4) occupational skill programs, in which
clients can learn trades and specific work skills. These usually
include janitorial, clerical, machine shop, electronic assembly,
and other manual types of skills. Facilities also have a host of
programs to accommodate severely disabled clients who are
mentally retarded or mentally ill, and who are incapable of
developing skills or tolerance to jobs. Programs for these clients
are termed work activities. Vocational rehabilitation funds are
not provided for these programs. County and state mental
health programs, United Way donations, and fees from families
and charitable organizations support such programs. Facilities
also receive fees paid by insurance companies to evaluate and
serve clients.

As the above illustrations of a workshop's programs show,
these facilities depend on a number of financial sources, private
and public, to serve clients. Facilities also subcontract work
projects from private industries in order to provide actual work
experiences for clients as well as to employ clients and to help
sustain the operating cost of the agency. The dual function of
facilities as providers of rehabilitation services and as employers
of the handicapped has created tensions that are discussed in
this study.

Importance of Workshops to This Study

Rehabilitation facilities play an important role in the vocational rehabilitation field for the following reasons: first,
rehabilitation facilities have and continue to represent a substantial fiscal and philosophical part of the VR program. Second,
the historical development of facilities since the 1960s represents
a series of political relationships and policy outcomes between
facility directors and public funding agency officials, chief of
whom have been VR state administrators. Also, workshops
have served an important role in rehabilitating clients received
from VR programs. Third, workshops are, for the most part,
private vendors dependent on public funding. An examination
of the strategic relationships between VR administrators and
facility directors, then, involves insights into policy implementation activities between the public and private sectors.

Historical Summary of Sheltered Workshops

The mission, role, and relationship of facilities to vocational rehabilitation programs has changed with federal VA legislation in general and with state VR administrators' strategies in particular. Leadership in the facility movement at the national and state levels has also been a powerful force in the success of workshops' ability to maintain their public funding base.

Workshop facilities in this country date to the 1800s. Such institutions serving the blind were the forerunners of this type of agency. Religious and charitable groups also originated and promoted facilities that employed the handicapped, usually on a long-term basis. Such organizations as Goodwill Industries, St. Vincent de Paul, and the Salvation Army were among the pioneers in this area. However, it was not until the mid-1950s that federal funding for the support of facility services began. The 1954 Rehabilitation Amendment, in particular, provided funds for this purpose. Wessen (1965:151) noted that a consequence of this federal act increased the number of clients served in rehabilitation workshops by over 300 percent.

The 1965 Rehabilitation Amendments authorized funds for the construction and staffing of workshops. Then in 1973, the Rehabilitation Act greatly aided workshops by enlarging the clientele vocational rehabilitation agencies would serve. The emphasis of this legislation was on severely disabled individuals— the population facilities had claimed to serve all along. With the 1978 amendments to the 1973 act, disabled clients without a vocational goal were, for the first time in the history of the vocational rehabilitation program, included as eligible VR participants.

Statistics from the U.S. Department of Labor reflect the increase in workshops and clients they serve. In 1954, 262 certified workshops served 15,237 clients. In 1975, 2,766 workshops served 116,947 clients (Greenleigh Associates 1975). By 1980 it is estimated that there were 6,000 rehabilitation facilities in the United States serving over 400,000 clients (Wright 1980). A 1977 U.S. Department of Labor study on workshops showed that a majority of the facilities were private corporations, and one-fourth were publicly operated (Wright 1980).

Among the major contributions workshops have made in serving disabled clients are the following: first, they have provided an alternative to long-term institutionalization of severely disabled persons in prisons and mental asylums; second, severely disabled clients have had the opportunity to develop skills and work tolerance to obtain competitive jobs. Very severely disabled individuals have been employed by workshops on a permanent basis. Third, workshops have demonstrated to private industry, government, and the public that mentally ill and retarded persons are vocationally productive if given the training opportunity in a supportive work environment.

Actual Controversies between Facilities and VR Administrators

Workshops' roles as employers and service providers have presented problems in that these facilities tend to displace their goals. Instead of serving severely disabled clients for employment in the external job market, workshops can select more productive clients and keep them working for a longer time in the agency's operations (Scott 1967). Since workshops are financially pressured as employers as well as service providers, they can pay clients lower wages in order to underbid other industries—and each other—to obtain subcontract work. Workshops may also underpay disabled clients by setting nondisabled productivity rates impossibly high or by underestimating the pay received by nondisabled workers. Such practices exploit disabled workers by preventing them from earning reasonable wages and from going into competitive employment. VR administrators have questioned the costs that workshop directors pass on to public funding agencies. Since most facilities earn a profit on the work clients produce, VR administrators have argued that part of this profit should help defray clients' rehabilitation costs. The extent to which workshop directors spread costs equitably among funding sources, clients' wages and their own overhead costs is controversial. Finally, workshops have been questioned about reinstitutionalizing clients; instead of clients serving as patients or inmates, the issue has been whether or not and to what extent they have become slave labor in such facilities. As stated earlier, these are controversial issues that are debated between VR administrators and workshop facility directors. Such issues have served as political weapons for VR administrators as well as legitimate attempts to assist clients.

The major importance of sheltered workshops to state VR administrators has been and is as follows: (1) they serve as primary industrial training centers for the very severely disabled clients who cannot obtain competitive employment; (2) they enable clients to remain in their communities while being trained; (3) they enable the very severely disabled a means of obtaining their independence and gaining vocational status in society. For these reasons, workshops represent a vital part of the VR services network.

4

Administrative Strategies during the Growth Period

Zealots are not extensive "imperialists"; rather,
they agitate for extremely intensive expansion of
a few policies. (Downs 1967: 110)

This chapter describes the intentional goal-attainment
activities of the first administrator in this study (Adams) and
his attempts to use external resources to impose his own strategies on the VR state policy arena during the period 1961-74.
Adams' leadership style and professional value orientation are
also examined in the context of the VR policy game played
between Adams and workshop directors. This chapter also
reconstructs the implemented policy outcomes and the observed
means Adams used to achieve his objectives. The observed
consequences of Adams' strategic activities on the organization,
on external organizational relations, and on vocational rehabilitation policy are discussed.

A major aim here is to identify what Miles (1982) stated
should be carried out in future organizational research, namely,

It is only through in-depth, real-time, action-
research focus that investigators will be able to
identify the powerful but sometimes subtle role of
executive leaders in developing, defining, and re-
inforcing the fit between the process of character
formation and strategy formation. These powerful
subtleties involve the creation of decision-making
settings, the framing of questions and symbols to
guide and reinforce problem-solving activity, the

selection of who will and will not be involved, the
sequencing and timing of these events to optimize
the potential of competing forces and uneven capa-
bilities within the enterprise, and the development
of knowledge and skills to manage the changing
configuration of organizational character, strategy,
and environment [p. 258]. To begin the following
guiding hypothesis was used to structure our
observations, administrative leaders who can successfully select and implement expansionist objectives
and strategies in an external environment characterized by growth increase the likelihood of enlarging
their organizational domains and operations.

We are particularly interested first in identifying the
sources and content of Adams' intentional or desired program
objectives and strategies he chose in order to respond to environmental trends during this period. Toward this end, these
questions focused our inquiry:

(1) What objectives and strategies were available from
Adams' perspective to gain control over the state VR policy
arena and to mobilize organizational members to accept and
implement them?
(2) What were the sources of the pressures in the policy
environment that influenced Adams to use particular external
strategies? Here we also ask, what were the characteristics of
Adams' leadership style that influenced his choice of objectives
and strategies?

It should be noted that Adams was actually the third
administrator of this state program. The first administrator
was considered the founder and missionary (Mintzberg 1983)
of the program both in this state and nationally. He had been
Adams' role model and mentor.
The second administrator held the post between 1951 and
1960. This person was observed to have been more of an arm
of the vocational educational program than a leader for the
vocational rehabilitation part of the system. Adams took over
the program after what many considered a decade of stagnation
for vocational rehabilitation in the state, at least as far as
obtaining autonomy and expansion for the VR program was
concerned. Adams told us that he considered his predecessor
too parochial and bureaucratic to innovate. Therefore, when
Adams took over the program his aim immediately became that

of returning it to the vision of greatness that the first director held. However, in 1961 the program was under the administrative umbrella of the state's vocational education board. Adams' notions of autonomy and expansion for the rehabilitation program were ahead of national growth trends in social services by at least five years. He was challenged with two factors that would constrain his expansive aims: a bureaucratic structure which housed his program and which had a vocational education director who was unsympathetic to giving power over to the rehabilitation part of the structure; and, an external national and state economic environment which at that time was not so responsive to expansion. Nevertheless, Adams geared up for expansion and he did so through a purposive set of intended strategies which he rigorously pursued for a decade.

Adams' Intended Strategic Responses

Adams developed at least three dominant policy objectives and several strategies over his term in order to gain autonomy and control federal resources for his program. We identified his objectives and strategies by using these methods: an extensive archival search of state agency records, interviews with Adams, and interviewing members of Adams' former staff. The criteria we used to identify Adams' intentional strategic plans were our reconstruction of Adams' own statement of his goals in available records; supporting evidence from Adams' staff who knew and described to us his intentional aims and evidence from external agency members who were involved with Adams in his policymaking plans and activities.

We found Adams' objectives and accompanying strategies to have been the following:

Intended objectives	Desired strategies
(1) Domain expansion:[1] Comprehensive VR program and direct client service policy expansion (1961-73).	(1-a) Cooperative partnership with private rehabilitation facility directors and their constituencies for political and program capacity support. (1-b) Development of relationships with national political figures to leverage state legislators' control of fiscal resources.

(2) Domain autonomy:
Increased administrative
discretion and organiza-
tional autonomy vis-à-vis
the state Vocational Edu-
cation Board (1966-68).

(3) Domain achievement:
National achievement and
recognition of state pro-
gram (1965-74)

(1-c) Manipulation of the overlapping federal/state
budget process.

(2-a) Alignment of the VR
program with the state
department of Health
and Human Services.

(2-b) Extension and diversification of staff to
increase administrative
turf.

(3-a) Emphasis and focus on
competitive program
achievement, measured
by the number of suc-
cessful rehabilitation
counselors obtained.

Domain Objectives and Strategies

While the concept of domain has been defined as the services
rendered by an organization, the technology used, and the
population served (Thompson 1967), we used the term to refer
to the policy spheres of influence that Adams intended to access
to control the distribution of federal funds in his state according
to his objectives; to choose the means and mechanisms by which
to allocate federal funds to structure his organization to serve
clients; and to determine the scope of services rendered.

Domain Expansion

Domain expansion refers to Adams' attempts to enlarge the
VR state program's funding, scope of services, clients, and
service vendors, such as rehabilitation workshops.

Adams sought to enlarge his programs primarily through
his personal and political contacts nationally and through his
association with workshop directors in the state. He informed
us that after he initially took office, he was anxious to get the
program back on track after ten years of fumbling around. He
said,

I had been frustrated with my predecessor's timid
approach with the state legislature. He would
always submit small budgets thinking he would get
in good with them. Meanwhile, our program was

going to hell. I turned things around. I told everybody, "Let's get federal money."

Adams initially sought to expand his access to available
federal funds. As early as 1961, he expressed this aim in a
request to the Vocational Education Board to whom he reported.
His request was recorded at a meeting.

Mr. Adams said that this year (1961) about three-
quarters of a million dollars of federal money available to the state will not be used because of
unavailable state matching funds. He said he was
advised that other states were using state funds
appropriated to other state agencies such as hospitals,
etc., to make federal allotments. Time studies have
been made of the activities of their professional
staffs to determine the amount of time spent in rehabilitation activities . . . if the state funds
specifically spent for these purposes could be
considered as state matching funds, additional
federal funds could be made available to this state,
which would enable us to expand our programs.
(State Vocational Educational Board Meeting Minutes,
volumes 11, 12, p. 210)

Adams was unsuccessful in his attempts to persuade the
Vocational Education Board to help him obtain more federal
funds for his and workshop programs that served VR clients.
He turned for political support to his friend Lands, a resident
of this state and a prominent ranking Republican minority
member of Congress's Finance Committee. According to Adams,

After I received token help from the Board and from
the federal rehabilitation office, I went to John
[Lands]. Together we worked out a draft amendment which stated that local communities could put
up their own match to get monies from the 1954
federal law. John got the amendment attached to
another bill and both passed.

The following exchange indicates the success of this venture
by Lands and Adams.

The Honorable John Lands
Member of Congress

House Office Building
Washington, D.C.
Dear John:

  The purpose of this letter is to express my
personal appreciation for the action you have taken
with regard to Vocational Rehabilitation Administration legislation. This change in vocational rehabilitation law is not only of tremendous benefit to our
state but to the nation. It will do more to give
impetus to the workshop movement and to the development of needed rehabilitation facilities than anything
since the 1954 amendments.

  You may be certain that the Vocational Rehabilitation Administration shares my enthusiasm and
gratitude for what you have done.

  I am making it my personal responsibility to let
the people of this state and my professional associates throughout the country know of the role
played by you in this matter.
Best personal regards,
Adams

Lands' response was a letter to Adams dated October 1964:

  Thank you for your note of October 14th. As you
know, my amendment was conceived and born in
the Hope County project office here in this state.
I hope other great things come from the Hope
County project office.
With best wishes and kindest personal regards,
I am,
John Lands

  Both Lands and Adams gained increased recognition from
the passage of this amendment: Lands from a new state constituency, and Adams from workshop directors in this state and
around the country.

  Adams' close relationship with noted professors in the
rehabilitation field at the state university also gained him
access to grant writing and research capability and thus additional federal program money.

  According to Adams in an interview for this study, he
and a state university professor thought up an interesting idea
while they were returning from Washington on a plane in the
early 1960s.

> We got the idea of trying the vocational rehabilita-
> tion case method approach to welfare clients. If our
> method could return welfare clients to work, the
> state would save money and the vocational rehabilita-
> tion philosophy of serving clients other than the
> physically and mentally disabled would be proven.
> After the second martini, the idea began to sound
> better and better. In fact, I decided to talk to
> Lands about it.

He persuaded Lands on the idea. As a result of Lands'
effort, in 1964 this state was awarded $5 million for a five-year
demonstration project that had the following goal:

> to examine the feasibility of expanding vocational
> rehabilitation services to the economically and
> socially disadvantaged as well as the physically
> and mentally disabled, and to provide services
> in a degree of saturation which would guarantee
> that all who needed vocational rehabilitation services
> in order to achieve employability would receive such
> services. (From a state vocational rehabilitation
> document entitled "Supporting Information, Hope
> County Rehabilitation Project As Requested by
> the Conference Committee on Finance")[2]

While Adams used innovation and his relationships with
Lands and the state university to secure federal funds, it was
his intended use of private rehabilitation facilities that was his
major strategy to directly access federal funds created by legislation during the Johnson administration.

The following excerpt of minutes taken at a 1965 Vocational
Education Board meeting showed that Adams intended to use
rehabilitation workshops to funnel federal funds into his program.
This quote also shows that he purposely pursued the Lands
Amendment to extend his own program potential through those
facilities.

> Mr. Adams said for many years we have had what
> we refer to as Section 2 funds which we were not
> able to match with state money and consequently
> each year this money lapsed. The Lands Amend-
> ment was passed by the last session of Congress
> which permits the matching of federal funds with
> local, private non-profit organization funds. This

provides a large source of previously untapped
money. The federal office solicited the states and
asked how much federal money would be needed to
carry on projects of this type. Our office in turn
asked the private organizations [rehabilitation
facilities] in the state if they would propose such
projects and on the basis of this information made
the best estimate possible. During the next fiscal
year approximately $20 million will be needed as a
very minimum to match contributions of private
organizations. As soon as this amendment became
known local and private organizations began in-
quiring relative to how they could take advantage
of these matching funds. . . .

Again, in his 1965 annual agency report, Adams emphasized
using rehabilitation workshops to respond to federal legislative
mandates to serve the severely disabled. His expansionist logic
regarding the use of workshops is explicitly revealed in this
statement:

The sheltered workshop remains the top prevocational
evaluation, work adjustment, and vocational training
resource for the mentally retarded. Vocational Rehabilitation as the principal purchaser of workshop
services has done much to stimulate the upgrading
of this important resource.
    Facilities for evaluation of the retarded are vital
to a successful rehabilitation program.
    Thirty work oriented rehabilitation facilities
in this state have an active working relationship
with the Rehabilitation Division. Because of vocational rehabilitation emphasis on service to the
severely disabled, the growth rate of sheltered
workshops in this state is one of the highest in
the nation, increasing by five per year. Only
two other states, Pennsylvania and Texas surpass
us in the number of vocational rehabilitation clients
in the work-oriented rehabilitation facilities.

Adams told us in an interview that during the 1960s rehabilitation workshops became the underground railroad through
which institutionalized offenders, the mentally ill, and emotionally
disturbed could escape back to society. He also repeatedly
emphasized in all our interviews his concern with expanding
these facilities.

Two major questions we asked, regarding Adams' strategic response to federal legislative and funding growth trends in general and through the use of workshops particularly, were: (1) Why did he adopt an expansionist objective, especially several years before the Great Society growth era began? and (2) Why did he select facilities as a major means to respond to environmental growth trends?

Adams used workshops, we found, because he knew the directors personally since he had worked with their programs and staff as a VR counselor; from 1961 to 1965 he needed the larger and more powerful urban facility directors' political support in Washington and in this state to leverage the legislature for matching funds; from 1966 to 1973, he needed program capacity, namely, space and training equipment to accommodate the increasing numbers of clients made eligible by federal VR legislation in the mid- to late 1960s.

Although Adams had the opportunity to build and run state-owned facilities in the late 1960s to train VR clients, he chose to use existing, privately run facilities because of his preoccupation with building the largest and most successful VR program in the country quickly, while federal funding was abundant. Moreover, because he had become politically aligned with facility directors early in his term, it was difficult for him to change policy directions and allegiances later.

Beyond these practical considerations, we argue from our observations and interviews that Adams' leadership style played a significant role in his choice of expansionist strategies. In particular, his charismatic style was repeatedly mentioned by almost everyone we interviewed as a dominant feature of his administration. In fact, those who worked closest to him called him a zealot. One of his top planners said he was an egotistical maniac.

It is important conceptually to link leadership style to an administrator's strategic choices and his/her predisposed way of reading and mapping an environment in which to implement those choices. Leadership style determines to a large extent the direction an administrator gives an organization and its activities. Given this reasoning, we look closer at the conceptual basis for our observations of Adams' style.

Charismatic Leadership Defined

Charisma has been identified more as a characteristic of founders, entrepreneurs, and missionary types of organizational leaders (Mintzberg 1983). Some writers have criticized the

mythical nature of charismatic leadership and have advocated
a more realistic view of leadership from a contingency perspective: that is, leaders do not guide or direct organizations so
much as manage several functions in them. Katz and Kahn
(1978), however, have directed attention back to the concept
of charisma as a descriptive characteristic for understanding
how top-level administrators perceive external opportunities
and shape policy accordingly. Charisma is, we contend, being
especially resourceful during growth periods, times when an
institutional perspective and wide-ranging skills, expertise,
and experience are needed to align the organization with changing external resources.

Katz and Kahn's definition of charisma is useful in its
application to organizational leadership style.

> Charisma is not the objective assessment by followers
> of the leader's ability to meet their specific needs.
> It is a means by which people abdicate responsibility
> for any consistent, tough-minded evaluation of the
> outcome of specific policies. (1978:545)

Katz and Kahn also state:

> The formulation of policy and the orientation of
> structure represent the kind of leadership acts
> most appropriate to charismatic leadership. The
> great majority of people are not in a position to
> evaluate proposals for major organizational change
> in any detail. They may or may not want to see
> social changes, and they may be sound in their
> judgment of overall goals, but they will not often
> be knowledgeable about specific programs to attain
> these goals. Hence, they will turn to the great
> leader whose character, strength, and skill give
> assurance that the problem will be solved. (1978:
> 546)

Adams admittedly learned the politics of the program from
the charismatic style of Bill, the first VR administrator. Adams
noted in an interview:

> Bill taught me the big picture of the program. He
> knew how the feds operated, how state legislators
> thought and how to put these parts of the puzzle

together to get the results he wanted. I learned
how legislation worked from him. I learned how
to figure the politics of the system and how to put
a plan into action. He was always a step ahead of
everybody else in knowing what he wanted and how
to get it.

Bill showed us that we had to fight for money
that was really ours. He used any method he could
to get our program going. He would join clubs, go
to business groups, anything to meet important
people.

Adams also related to us that Bill used his staff to establish
and promote the first VR program in the state. From these
experiences Adams admitted that he learned the program
thoroughly, and that he gained a view of vocational rehabilitation
as it operated nationally and in the states.

Adams' Professional Background and Value Orientation

George Wright (1980:165) asserted that

the most successful administrators of state rehabilitation agencies are career professionals who started
as field counselors and have been gradually promoted through the ranks of supervision and management of the agency.

Adams was a career VR professional who lived and worked
in this state all his life. His orientation to the field through
counselling remained a major source of his leadership motivation
and professional value orientation.

Even as Adams progressed through the ranks as supervisor
and then administrator, his contact with counselors and field
supervisors was regularly maintained. The most senior management staff member who had worked the longest with Adams
commented,

Adams was a program zealot. Everything he thought
about had to do with the program. At every meeting we talked about clients, counselors. If you
wanted to get him excited, you just started talking
about stories involving either politics about the
program or about clients.

Adams' Leadership Style

When asked at two meetings to explain his leadership style during his administration, particularly in terms of how he guided the agency from 1961 through 1974, Adams responded,

> First, I want to say three things that I think made
> me successful: the first was my knowledge of the
> program, since I worked with it most of my life;
> the second was my ability to persuade people—
> anybody—to get what I wanted; and I also had the
> guts to do what I believed was right.
> My predecessor (the second administrator)
> was timid about the political process and he didn't
> know the program. He already had two strikes
> against him.
> You see, I didn't have gun barrel vision.
> I saw the program from my experience of working
> in it. I knew what was good for the program and
> I knew how to get it.

Adams also noted,

> I used my own money to take legislators, board
> members, bureaucrats out for drinks and dinners
> to get my ideas and plans across. And when I
> hit the road, I went to get to know the people we
> were serving as well as to find out what we were
> doing. I enjoyed going into facilities and talking
> with the floor workers as well as the directors.
> I bet I got more money and favors for the program
> over fishing trips and card games than I did at
> any of the congressional hearings and meetings
> with the state legislative committees.

As Pfeffer has noted (1981), "Individual resources and abilities can impact the power exercised by the occupant of a given structural position." Bucher (1970:30), cited by Pfeffer, also noted in a study of power in a hospital;

> The major consequence of assessed stature is that
> it affects a person's ability to negotiate and persuade
> successfully, and it is primarily through negotiation
> and persuasion that the decisions that carry forward
> the work of the organization are made. (1970:3)

Bucher concluded:

> Does participation in an extensive network of relation-
> ships both inside and outside the department consti-
> tute in itself a source of power? The data suggest
> that extensiveness of role-set is a necessary but
> not insufficient condition for power, and that
> assessed stature is the more critical variable.
> (1970:37)

Our interviews with Adams and those who knew and
worked with him support Bucher's findings. Adams' sense of
self-confidence in his leadership role and position was rooted
in his program knowledge and experience. He exerted tremendous
influence by persuading and negotiating his demands into action.

He saw himself as the legitimate leader-statesman (in
Selznick's terms) of the VR program. He embodied the mission
of the program. He believed in his political and program capability. His sense of self-confidence and commanding way of
administering the program led him to become autocratic and
arbitrary in his internal organizational control strategies and
in his perception of external events.

To understand Adams' other intended objectives (i.e.,
domain autonomy and achievement) and the strategies he sought
to implement these objectives, it is necessary to turn to his
relations with workshop (facility) directors in the state. It
was with and through his games with these directors that Adams
looked to extend his program and his own power.

The Policy Game between Adams and
Rehabilitation Facilities

The metaphor of game has been used to examine interactions
and relationships within and between organizations (Allison
1971; Bardach 1977; Crozier and Friedberg 1977). This perspective is particularly useful here because it helps us to
explain external events as these were mediated through the
strategies and interactions of Adams and key facility directors.
The demands and interests of facility directors are also important
to understand since these impinged on Adams' domain objective
of expansion in particular. To begin this part of the discussion,
we introduce the facility directors as the other major players
in this state's VR policy arena.[3]

ACTORS IN THE GAME: REHABILITATION
FACILITY DIRECTORS, THE METROPOLITANS,
AND THE RURALS

In 1961 there were fewer than 20 private rehabilitation
facilities in this state. By 1966 the number had increased to
30, and by 1974 there were 47. As was the situation in other
states, private rehabilitation workshops could be differentiated
between those located in metropolitan areas and the majority,
which were situated in outlying and rural regions. The metropolitans (the term we use for the urban directors) generally
wielded more political power and received more of the state
human service agencies' fiscal resources than all of the rurals
combined. This was the case for two reasons: first, the metropolitans had a larger population of clients from which to select
and serve; second, these facility directors were more adept at
developing political networks among state and big city politicians
and legislators.

The Metropolitans

The three most politically influential urban-based facility
directors during the growth period all ran workshops in the
state's single largest city, Seaside. Their combined budgets
commanded more than one-third of Adams' allocation to all direct
client services.
These three facilities had the most sophisticated training
equipment and the most space for dealing with clients. They
also had the most impressive placement records for obtaining jobs
for clients since they had a larger range of business contacts.
The most politically active and vocal of the three metropolitans was Gates. He had become a nationally known figure
in the rehabilitation field. He ran one of the oldest and most
widely recognized private facilities in the nation. He had gained
recognition for taking any client regardless of the client's disability or potential for rehabilitation.
His influence was visible in the state's legislature, in
Seaside's political circles, and in national politics. For example,
he produced letters at our interview from President Kennedy,
who had praised him for his professional efforts. Gates also
had helped Kennedy obtain suitable living arrangements for
Kennedy's disabled sister.
Of the 16 facility directors we interviewed who knew and
had worked with Gates between 1961 and 1974, there was

unanimous agreement that he was representative of their demands during most of that period. One director of another populous city informed us that he had openly differed with Gates on his approach and tactics during parts of this period.

Also, in our search through the official minutes of the Board of Vocational Education's meetings between 1950 to 1974, Gates' speeches, addresses, and comments were the most prominent of the facility directors. For these reasons, we refer to him in these sections as representative of the metropolitans in their collective interactions with Adams.

The Rurals

The rural and non-metropolitan based facility directors numbered 14 in 1961 and more than 40 by 1974. However, their individual budgets ranged only between $50,000 and $1 million. These directors spent less time campaigning for political and economic support and were more involved in the daily operations of their facilities. We also observed that the rurals resented the urban directors' control of state fiscal resources. (We noticed how this resentment was quickly abandoned when both groups were faced with economic, political, or program policy issues that could unite them.)

While rural facilities were not as immediately important politically to Adams as the metropolitans, the rurals enabled him to show state and federal legislators that his operation indeed was statewide. Programmatically, the rural facilities also offered Adams the only source of training for disabled clients in many outlying areas.

Most of the rural directors were his friends. He fished with many of them and frequently visited their workshops. The majority of rural facility directors we interviewed remembered Adams as a friend and partner in the rehabilitation process. Different directors repeatedly recalled their direct contact with him, his personal visits to and concern with their work areas, and his impressive political clout in support of their cause. All evaluated him more favorably than they did his successors. It was not until the early 1970s that many of the rural facility directors aligned with the metropolitans against Adams' policies.

Adams' Reconstructed Position in the Game with Facilities

Between 1961 and 1965 the major position Adams adopted in his use of facilities to expand his program was the following:

How to use grassroots facility political support to access available but procedurally restrictive federal funds in order to leverage both the state legislature and the Vocational Education Board to submit optimal matching monies for rehabilitation programs.

Adams, for example, told us

I wanted a partnership with facilities. I wanted them as an ally representing local communities. When I went before the state Finance Committee to argue my case for the match, I could call on facilities to bring their clients and testify. They brought clients in wheelchairs and crutches. It worked.

Adams also recalled that Gates helped align congressional support to help with the passage of the Lands Amendment.

Gates did his part in Seaside and in Washington. We knew that if this amendment passed, we all would gain. We worked as a team in those days. I wanted a strong program and facilities needed clients.

Excerpts from our interviews with three state legislators, who served on the powerful Finance Committee, also indicated their awareness of Adams' coalition with Gates.

First Legislator: I remember Adams would present his statistics and funding needs and then call on Gates who was the more eloquent of the two. Gates had a way of trying to commit everybody to his cause.

Second Legislator: Adams was an enthusiast who always wanted us to help bring federal money into the state. He used every means he could to make a case. He and the facility people would parade crippled people into the chamber before they made their presentations. It usually worked.

Third Legislator: Legislators think they can structure things in a way that administrators have to carry out our intent. It didn't work that way. If legislators are ahead of bureaucrats and administrators, then administrators lose some power. Administrators like the one you are talking about from vocational rehabilitations used community groups to back his cause. He knew how to work the system.

The director of the Vocational Education Board during that period also informed us in an interview that Adams and Gates met regularly with the governor and with members of the Board to influence their decisions to increase vocational rehabilitation funding and programming.

> Adams and Gates were always up to something. They held a meeting with the governor and invited me to attend. The agenda turned out to be a discussion of federal funds that could be brought into the state with adequate matches. I saw the game they were up to.
> I had to keep a step ahead of them with Board members. They lobbied everybody they could to favor the vocational rehabilitation program and facilities.

Adams' Tactics in the Game

We hypothesized in Chapter 2 that

> Major external negotiation tactics based on cooperation will enable administrators to successfully select and implement strategies to enlarge their organization during external growth periods.

Evidence presented above supports this statement. Adams and Gates, in particular, worked closely together to pressure the state legislature and the Vocational Education Board to match and obtain available federal funds for the VR program and facilities.

Another significant example of cooperative coalition-building activities between Adams and Gates is illustrated in the following exchange of letters. The first was dated February 3, 1965, and was sent to Adams from Gates.

> Dear Mr. Adams:
> May I express my sincere congratulations on the very effective job you did which resulted in the wonderful material that the Governor included in his budget message. The material is so encouraging that it will be enthusiastically received by all parent groups and all of us in the field of vocational rehabilitation.

I, personally, know how much this message
depended on the work that you did. I think you
deserve a great deal of credit for this tremendous,
progressive step that is being taken in the field of
vocational rehabilitation. May I offer you my sincer-
est congratulations, and assure you of my cooperation in the substantial work that remains to be
done to carry out the objectives you have set for
the rehabilitation programs in our state.
                                                Cordially,
                                                Gates

The return letter dated February 26, 1965, is from Adams to
Gates:

Dear Mr. Gates:
        Thank you for your kind letter of February 3.
You will be pleased to know that we have had favor-
able hearings with both the Governor and the Joint
Committee on Finance. There is every indication
that we will enjoy a substantial budget increase for
the coming biennium.
        Best personal regards.
                                                Sincerely yours,
                                                Adams

End of the Honeymoon

        The honeymoon period (1961-65) between Adams and work-
shop directors was initiated by Adams early in his term in order
to win facility political support to leverage state legislators and
the Vocational Education Board to expand VR program matching
funds. Adams and the facility directors found a common enemy
in the Board and in state legislators who served as barriers
for them to access maximum VR funds in the early to mid-1960s.
However, the coalition between Adams and the metropolitan
facility directors, in particular, became strained as Adams
began to respond to federal trends to expand his own power
base beyond rehabilitation facility support.
        Adams altered his strategic focus from the political use
of facilities to an emphasis on programs as events changed
from the mid- to late 1960s. Our reconstruction of his position
change from the evidence we gathered in interviews and official
reports can be summarized as follows:

Increase program use of facilities to accommodate federal mandates for serving a wider range of clients without sharing more control of VR client policy or funding decisions with workshop directors.

External Federal Events that Influenced Adams' Position Shift

Adams decreased his dependence on and use of workshops in his expansionist program strategies for the following reasons. First, between 1965 and 1974 Adams developed a broader power base from which to access federal funds. For example, the director of the federal vocational rehabilitation office became czar of a newly created federal super agency which administered the full range of human services in the country. Adams and this director became close friends as well as professional associates. Her promotion to head the new agency increased Adams' political access to federal legislators and bureaucrats. Adams told us

> Mary [the federal VR administrator] would invite me with other congressmen to have dinner in her private quarters below her office. We talked about ways to get backing for bills and funds to the states. She used me to pass on success stories about clients in the state that legislators could use in their speeches. I travelled to Washington frequently and got involved in the politics down there through her.

Second, 1965 VR legislation increased the federal funding share to 75 percent with a 25 percent required state match funding. In 1968, the federal share was changed to 80 percent with a 20 percent state matching requirement. For Adams, these new funding ratios created more incentive as well as increased pressure on his state's legislature to bring in federal funds. Adams continued to struggle with state legislators to obtain funding matches, but by 1967 he had developed more support from different political bases.

Third, the growth of federal VR funding coupled with legislative changes that increased client eligibility standards also changed Adams' game plan from one of having to concentrate on politically accessing funds and promoting programs to that of accommodating the growth trends. Space and training opportunities for clients became central issues.

Fourth, 1965 federal VR legislation provided state programs for the first time since their inception with the legal opportunity to separate from vocational education boards by joining other units of state government. Adams had the chance to decrease his reliance on the state vocational education board's conservative administrative authority and policies.

Adams' Responses to External Changes

During the mid-1960s, Adams responded to these events by pursuing domain autonomy and domain achievement objectives simultaneously with domain expansion. Adams' expanded power base, combined with easier access to more abundant federal funds, led him to seek more individual position power and organizational autonomy. Adams changed his tactics from cooperation to control and even competition with facilities in his attempt to use their physical space and programs without sharing program policy and funding decisions.

According to our interviews with Adams, he sought domain autonomy for the VR program as a primary objective for these reasons: first, Adams had been constrained by the vocational education board director's conservative fiscal and program philosophy regarding vocational rehabilitation. This tension intensified as federal VR funding increased. As stated earlier, Adams blamed this director and the second VR administrator for the loss of millions of available federal dollars for the VR program even during the 1950s.

Second, as Adams succeeded in accessing federal funds with the help of facility directors and other powerful political figures, he wanted more individual credit and recognition for his efforts. He told us in an interview

> Fred [the vocational educational director] didn't like or really want to lobby legislators for program funds, but once the money was approved he wasn't shy to take credit for it.

Third, Adams and members of his staff during that period also expressed dissatisfaction and disapproval with the philosophy and practice of the vocational educational system. They saw vocational rehabilitation methods as distinct from and often in conflict with practices in educational rehabilitation. Adams, for example, told us

> I had counselors telling me they would refer clients for vocational training in one of the state schools

and the clients would last a couple of weeks. They
couldn't handle the classroom situation or the higher
level teaching. I discussed these issues with Fred
[the vocational director], to get him to develop
programs for more severely handicapped clients.
I don't think he knew how or could.

Federal and State Events Influencing
Adams' Autonomy Objective

Between 1965 and 1967, events at the federal and state
government levels opened the way for Adams to assert his
drive for organizational and administrative autonomy. The
1965 federal VR Act permitted the state education agency (or
an agency of two or more organizational units that administered
one or more public education, health, welfare or state labor
programs) to administer the VR program. Also, during this
same time, the governor had commissioned a study of the
human service programs in the state. The conclusion of the
study (the "Kelson Report") stated that there was a waste of
resources, lack of coordination, and duplication of social service
programs and funding in the state. The report recommended
a department be formed to consolidate and coordinate these
programs. The recommendation was adopted and the new
agency was named the Department of Health and Social Services
(DHSS). Adams finally had a rationale to separate from the
vocational education system.
We asked Adams what his intended purposes for joining
DHSS were. He responded,

My goal was to get closer to state legislators and
other social services program directors in the state
who were lobbying and getting more state funds
than I could with the Board. I was always two
steps removed from the funding action. I had to
go through the Board to get to the legislators.

He continued,

I moved our program into DHSS because the vocational educational system was stagnating under
Fred (the director) who was an ultra-conservative
guy. Besides, the correctional program, mental
health services, welfare—all these were in the
Health and Social Services agency; we fit into
that group more than with education.

Adams also said that he could manipulate two budgets (the federal and state) once he was outside the control of the vocational education board, where he had had little control over the VR budget, except to lobby for matching funds and submit requests.

Adams told us he had a friend, Ben, in the state Department of Administration who was responsible for monitoring and approving other state agencies' funding requests before these were sent for legislative review. Adams said:

> Ben was appointed as our budget analyst if and
> when we decided to go with DHSS. I checked with
> him about our joining. I asked him if I would have
> leeway in lobbying and getting more state funds.
> He agreed the new setup would probably be better
> for us. From that discussion I learned that I had
> another ally in a position that counted.

Adams also informed us that once inside DHSS,

> I figured I could take advantage of overlapping state
> and federal budget periods. The federal budget was
> out before the state funds were allocated. I knew if
> I asked for and got more state matching funds than
> I needed for the federal share, I could use the state
> match to capture unspent federal monies from other
> states. That's what happened for years. Even
> Ben didn't really catch on to what I was doing
> until late in the game.

Adams' intentions for joining the new Department of Health and Social Services, then, fit his objectives of domain expansion and autonomy. However, Adams had not anticipated the longer-term consequences his move to the department would produce. His organizational autonomy and administrative discretion became strained within the changing administrative leadership of DHSS.

ADAMS' RESPONSES TO EXTERNAL
GROWTH TRENDS

Domain Achievement

It is difficult to say exactly when Adams adopted and articulated a domain achievement objective for his program. After reviewing our interviews with Adams and the historical data we collected on the VR agency during that period, we concluded that Adams was probably motivated from the beginning of his term toward program achievement. His charismatic style, as we indicated earlier, influenced the orientation of his program objectives in expansionist and achievement directions. However, we found that his achievement objective became more competitively oriented between the mid- to late 1960s.

Our evidence indicated that Adams began to equate program achievement quantitatively, that is, with numbers of successfully rehabilitated clients in the state and with the national ranking of the program with regard to successful rehabilitations. He recorded in his 1966 annual agency report:

> The remarkable success and growth of vocational rehabilitation in recent years speak well for the wisdom of Solomon. This state's vocational rehabilitation program today still does not have "a multitude of counselors" but it does have nearly 100 with the skills necessary to lift the "fallen," be it from physical, mental or social causes. Nationally, there continues to be an annual shortage of more than 1,200 counselors and in the state, counselor recruitment is always in progress. During fiscal 1966, vocational rehabilitation increased its counseling staff by 25. This added counselor strength made possible the most successful year thus far in this state's vocational rehabilitation history. Nearly 4,600 handicapped persons entered employment after receiving evaluation, counseling, training, physical restoration and/or job placement services through the Rehabilitation Division. This represents an increase of 41 percent over the total for 1965, a 200 percent increase over 1961. Our vocational rehabilitation program recorded the nation's best percentage increase for agencies rehabilitating 1,000 or more clients in 1966, 27 percent above the national average.

Adams seemed obsessed with being number one among other states in terms of numbers of successfully rehabilitated clients. We asked him if he had used competitive ranking of his program as a major indicator of achievement and success. He replied,

> People would always say to me at the national meetings, "How come Georgia could rehabilitate 5,000

clients in a year and our state only 1,000?" We
found out we could too.

I wasn't naive. I knew what the "Feds"
counted as successful—numbers. If you wanted
money, recognition and status nationally, you
turned in the numbers. The year I left the agency,
the total number of people rehabilitated was over
1,000.

Adams' assistant administrator, a career VR professional,
also reflected on the agency's achievement orientation:

Between 1921 and 1973, rehabilitation administrators
got into the rut of accounting for successful rehabilitations. We kept clients that were less
expensive to close. That way we spread our funds
out further to cover more clients who could be
rehabilitated. In a sense, we just complied with
what the system rewarded. Adams was just more
zealous in his approach to be number one.

This particular objective and practice of Adams' administration agitated rehabilitation facility directors because they
were prevented from keeping productive clients in their operations. They therefore lost money and reliable labor by the
quick turnover of clients. They also complained that Adams'
practice of "creaming" clients (preselecting those who would
be successfully rehabilitated) was unlawful and against rehabilitation norms. Consequently, over time the relationship
between Adams and the metropolitans became more strained.

Adams' Change in Tactics with Facility Directors:
From a Political to a Programmatic Emphasis

From our reconstruction of Adams' perspective, facilities
became more a means to his ends instead of allies working toward
common goals. Facilities had served a crucial political function
between 1961 and 1965 by helping Adams leverage the rigid
vocational education board and the state legislature for increased
funds. Both Adams and facility directors had gained in this
venture. However, as Adams succeeded in gaining organizational
autonomy and broader political support systems, he also began
to minimize the partnership aspect of his relationship with facilities. Facilities still had a dominant strategic role for Adams;
but, in the late 1960s, Adams tried to reduce their importance
to the role of service providers.

Interviews with members of Adams' top-level management staff who related to facility directors reflected Adams' strategic and tactical shift toward facilities. Adams' assistant administrator stated in an interview:

> Gates and others started telling us they could do
> the job of our counselors better. They wanted us
> just to give them the money and leave them alone.
> The truth was, they wanted to have all our client
> referrals. We had to get tough with some of the
> larger facilities, or else we would have spent all
> our budget in those places. Our job was to direct
> policy and distribute funds.

Oakes, Adams' workshop bureau director at that time, stated:

> We had a hell of a time keeping facilities honest
> during this period. They wanted everything they
> could get from the agency. I started the negotia-
> tions with 15 facilities in the state in the early
> 1960s. We first used a fee-for-services payment
> system with them; we would send clients in for
> service and pay for what they received. In the
> late 1960s, I started a simple contracting system
> with facilities. There were less than 30 of them
> in those days. We would try to figure out what
> our fair share of their costs would be for providing
> service to DVR clients. In the early 1970s, we
> went back to a fee-for-services system. We had
> a difficult time paying only our earned costs for
> services. Then again in 1974, we established
> another contracting system. It was hard with
> any system we used in those days. We all knew
> the real issue was power, not just programs.

Adams also noted:

> Some of the facility directors started getting greedy.
> Gates thought he was Mr. Rehabilitation in the
> state. I admired him but I also had my job to do.
> I wasn't going to turn the program over to Gates
> or any of those guys. And I didn't. We gave
> and took some punches over our negotiations with
> them.

FACILITY DIRECTORS' POSITION

Of the metropolitans, Gates' written and recorded communications to Adams and the Board were the most numerous, articulate, and outspoken. Of the three major metropolitan directors, Gates also wielded the most power in Washington circles and with state legislators. He was also well respected among his peers.

While Adams and members of his staff held that facility directors—Gates and the metropolitans especially—desired political control over VR state policy and funding decisions, Gates articulated a different view. His and other facility directors' position was:

> To survive, facilities needed guaranteed income,
> the majority of which should come from VR funding,
> to train handicapped clients. Low level client
> productivity was inadequate to cover the costs
> to run facilities. Facilities also needed policies
> from the VR agency which stated the length of
> time, payments, types of services and agreed on
> outcomes of clients in workshops.

Because workshops had to bid for jobs from industries, facility staff had to calculate their costs to cover all expenses in advance. These costs included anticipated client wages, training materials, and other operating expenses. Client inefficiency, absenteeism, and turnover represented major costs that were difficult to predict. Facility directors claimed that the uncertainties and competitiveness of the industrial and economic environment in which facilities had to participate to win bids to provide work for clients, required policy and funding assurances from public sector agencies.

In an extended interview with Gates, the underlying logic of the facility directors' position toward Adams regarding these issues was articulated.

> Adams had no policy on workshops. We had to
> force policies on him. I fought with Adams, not
> the agency's mission. It was Adams who directed
> his counselors to cream clients because it is
> cheaper. Our policy has always been to take any
> handicapped client who needed training or just a
> place to work. Sure it's costly, who said it wasn't?
> But we as rehab professionals create the problems.

We sell the notion that all handicapped people can
become happy and independent. But that's a lie.
So many severely disabled people can never work
productively or independently. Then what should
we do? Throw them in the streets because we can't
show a successful rehabilitation? It was never the
workshop's purpose to pay people enough to be
independent. Workshops must be inefficient operations. We take people industries don't want. What
do we get for it? Problems from the state agency
for not performing miracles, a bad image in society
because any institutions that have unhappy people
have bad societal images.

None of the vocational rehabilitation administrators have told us, we want peace, we want
realistic services, we want to share your resources.
They all have wanted only success stories, to help
us with our fiscal records. I blame them for not
spending federal money to improve the technology
to help handicapped people. Instead, they compete with the vocational technical schools to get
rehabilitated clients on the records. They have
their own agendas and goals which are not related
to helping handicapped persons.

Excerpts from Gates' letter (December 3, 1965) to Adams
almost two decades before this excerpt also reflected facility
directors' concerns with Adams' attitude toward workshops:

A policy from your office which would authorize a
maximum amount of training for every individual,
no matter how severely handicapped, would be in
line with the needs of the severely handicapped
mentally ill and mentally retarded. I feel that this
is in line with the new legislation and the increased
funds that are being made available to the states,
and I would sincerely appreciate your establishing
such a policy so that each individual rehabilitation
worker would not be in position to act on the basis
of previous policy determinations and, therefore,
bring about a situation where an individual has
the extent of his services decided by the personal
policy interpretations of an individual worker or
individual office. . . . I would sincerely appreciate
your office establishing a policy consistent with the
federal government's policy under its new legisla-

tion of an 18-month eligibility for continuing
services for severely handicapped mentally retarded
and emotionally disturbed. May I express my sincere
appreciation for your consideration of our problem.

The facility directors in the state also had to respond to
changing federal legislation and funding trends for organizational
survival and growth. While our interviews with the metropolitan
directors indicated that they also sought power and prestige,
still they had to operate physical plants and training programs
which required funding. They therefore needed a certain
guaranteed level of income to maintain requested program levels
sought by Adams and his counseling staff. Since guaranteed
income levels and fixed policies on VR client related services
in facilities were not forthcoming from Adams to the satisfaction
of most facility directors, they used other tactics to cover their
operating costs and to survive and thrive in the competitive
and uncertain industrial environment in which they operated.
The tactics facility staff used are briefly described below.

Twelve (of eighteen) facility staff members across the
state with whom we conducted interviews and held informal
discussions admitted to selecting and maintaining workers
(clients) in workshops who were more productive than others.
One floor supervisor in the largest facility in the state told us:

Let's be realistic, we have to cover our costs otherwise we couldn't stay in business. If funding
agencies subsidized the inefficiencies of lower level
clients, then we wouldn't have to cover our costs
by selecting and keeping the best workers. But
they don't. The burden is left with us. We all
have to keep a good mix between productive and
unproductive clients.

Scott (1967) described this selection and hiring process
in workshops for the blind from the perspective of goal
displacement—that is, leaders articulate one set of goals but
actually pursue others. From our interviews with workshop
employers and supervisors, we found this process to have been
an intended although inexplicit goal, which was adopted largely
as a reaction to arbitrary and undesirable policies from the VR
state agency. Workshop directors also had to adjust and excel
in a competitive industrial environment.

The expectation of facility directors to have most if not
all of their operating costs covered by public funds was un-
acceptable to Adams. He maintained that the metropolitan facility

directors, in particular, wanted to make money to expand their own salaries and operations on client labor. He was opposed to facility directors' attempts to have the state pay for all the training costs of clients. Facility directors therefore manipulated pay rates as a means to pass on inefficiency costs to other sources.

Another major but unofficial tactic we found that some workshops in the state used was that of underestimating both disabled and nondisabled workers' pay rates in facilities.

Freedman and Keller (1981:452) cited the Wall Street Journal investigation (1979) into this practice used by workshops across the country.

> The Journal reports that some of the 3,500 workshops, farms, and factories certified to pay according to productivity may be exploiting the handicapped by setting nonhandicapped productivity rates impossibly high or by underestimating the pay received by nonhandicapped workers. Thus, approximately 200,000 handicapped individuals employed in such concerns may be prevented from earning a reasonable wage and from moving into a competitive position where earnings would be higher and independence more likely.

Our interviews with a Department of Labor employee who came to the state during our study and who was responsible for checking and enforcing violations of pay rates such as those listed above, informed us:

> We don't have enough resources or manpower to actually go into every workshop and check their records and correlate their records with actual client hours. We have to take the word of facilities that they are doing the best they can according to the laws and conditions which they work under.
>
> The truth also is, we just haven't enforced this area of the law because it is kind of fuzzy and because of the nature of these institutions. They're not industries and they're not welfare agencies, they're doing the work of both.

Given these governmental gaps in developing and enforcing client wage regulating, facility directors in this state adopted practices that protected and advanced their own economic, political, organizational, and individual interests in a public and private sector environment characterized as competitive, uncoordinated, and somewhat Darwinian in nature.

POLICY OUTCOMES

We now turn to a reconstruction and discussion of the outcomes and policies resulting from Adams' relationship with facilities and from his intended aims. In this section we present data which are used to reflect on the extent to which Adams succeeded in achieving his goals based on expansion, organizational autonomy, and program achievement.

Evidence obtained regarding increases between 1961 and 1974 in Adams' program expenditures, staff, and clients rehabilitated indicated the statistical success of his intended expansion.

Table 4.1 shows the absolute dollar increases in this state's staff and program expenditures between the following years: 1961, 1965, 1969, 1970, and 1974. These figures are gross indicators of Adams' fiscal program growth, since adjustments using real dollar increases controlling for inflation rates were not available.

There was an increase of 126 percent of the total program expenditures between 1961 and 1965, a few years before the actual Great Society legislation and funding was implemented. Between 1965 and 1970, the height of the Johnson administration,

TABLE 4.1

State VR Staff and Program Expenditures, 1961-74

	Total Staff Expenditures	Program and Client-Related Expenditures	Total
1961	420,044	927,383	1,347,427
1965	788,879	2,258,673	3,047,552
1969	2,570,287	9,573,410	12,143,697
1974	7,032,327	16,006,266	23,038,593

Source: DVR Budgets, state archives.[4]

there was a 319 percent increase in Adams' total program expenditures. Between 1970 and 1974, the years designated as a slowdown or stabilized growth period for VR funding during the Nixon administration, Adams' program expenditures increased by 80 percent.

The expansion of the state's expenditures between 1961 and 1974 was substantial as compared to national total expenditures of all state VR programs. Table 4.2 illustrates the percentage increases of the program as compared with national expenditures between 1961 and 1974. The percentage increases of administrative and field staff salaries in this program are also shown during the same time period. National comparison statistics were not available to illustrate staffing increases.

In addition to the increases in management and field staff expenditures as presented above, we also point out that in 1950 this program had 32 employees. By 1961 that number increased only to 41. However, between 1965 and 1974, the

TABLE 4.2

State VR Program Expenditures Compared with National Expenditures

	Years	
	Great Growth Period (1961-69)	Stabilized Growth Period (1970-74)
Percentage increase in state agency's total expenditures (%)	801	80
Increase in national programs total expenditures (%)	417	45
Increase in state agency's administrative staff expenditures (%)	1,018	100
Increase in state agency's direct service staff expenditures (%)	471	74

Source: State and federal annual vocational rehabilitation statistical reports.

TABLE 4.3

Number of Clients Rehabilitated, with National Rank of VR
Agencies, 1961-69

Year	Rehabili- tations	Rate per 100,000	National Rank
1961	1577	40	37
1962	1864	46	31
1963	2225	54	23
1964	2684	66	21
1965	3293	80	19
1966	4556	111	13
1967	6115	148	11
1968	7289	174	8
1969	8693	208	8

Source: VR agency documents in state historical archives.

end of Adams' term, the agency's staff had grown to almost
600 employees. During his administration Adams had assembled
a prolific management bureaucracy along with a substantial
field counseling staff component.

In the 1969 agency Annual Report a profile of the number of rehabilitations and the rate per 100,000 were listed and
ranked nationally (Table 4.3).

The growth and success of the program as measured
numerically are evident from these statistics.

Adams responded to changing federal legislative mandates
to serve a wider range of more severely disabled clients between 1968 and 1972 by opening the doors to public offenders
and other behavioral disability groups. Table 4.4 shows the
increase in the number of these disability groups and the
percentage of these rehabilitated clients compared to total
client rehabilitations.

While these statistics show the impressive gains in the
number of rehabilitations and new clients served, they do not
reflect the unwritten policies and the political outcomes of
Adams' activities. Below, we discuss our reconstruction of
the political results of Adams' expansionism regarding his
client services policy.

TABLE 4.4

Profile of Rehabilitation Percentages of Public Offender and
Behavior Disabilities

| | State Agency Fiscal Year | | | | |
	1968	1969	1970	1971	1972
Public offender and other behavioral disabilities rehabilitated	795	1217	1324	1574	1795
Percentage of total rehabilitated	11	14	14.74	16.95	18.10

Source: State agency Annual Reports, 1968-72.

Interviews with eight of Adams' former field counseling
supervisors led to the conclusion that Adams' policy to accommodate more severely disabled clients, as the federal acts mandated,
was geared more toward increasing body counts and obtaining
successful rehabilitations than meeting the intent of the law.
We quote briefly excerpts from these interviews to illustrate
the common themes expressed by those interviewed:

Supervisor A: We were told to get out there and close [rehabili-
tate] clients who wouldn't drain our funds. After ten years
in this business, you can feel by talking with a client for
15 minutes whether or not he can be closed and almost what
it will cost.
Supervisor B: "Low caseloads don't correlate with high closures,"
we were told. So we increased our referrals among inmates,
and other clients who were trainable and employable and
who we could write up as having some behavioral disability.
In those days, we didn't have to use our imagination to make
a client eligible; the laws did it for us.
Supervisor C: Adams assigned me to correctional institutions.
My job was to refer inmates scheduled to complete their time
into our program. My understanding was to pick the winner.

Adams also substantiated the above findings, when he stated in an interview:

> We placed counselors in every correctional institution
> in the state. The federal law said clients had to
> have an emotional, mental or behavioral impediment
> to be eligible in our program. We got legal advice
> in Washington and tried rehab in corrections,
> hospitals, and mental institutions. Within two
> years, we had 8,000 clients from these places.
> In a way, it was easier to get clients from these
> sources than from the community. The numbers
> speak for themselves.

We discovered that the major criticism of facilities by Adams and many of his staff was evident in their own practice of pre-selecting or "creaming" clients who could increase the statistical success rate of the program.

Concluding Comments

From these results it is evident that Adams' own program interests of expansion were basically satisfied and that facility programs were substantially enhanced.

Closely related to Adams' intended objective of domain expansion was his aim to gain national recognition for his program achievements.

We asked Adams in a concluding interview for the study, what would you list as your major achievements as administrator of the program? He responded:

> First, I helped get the Lands Amendment passed.
> Lands and I both were proud of this. I also got
> the $5 million dollar project going (even though I
> don't think it would have worked nationally). I
> built two facilities in the state and helped all of
> them build their programs.
> The year I left, the total number of people
> rehabilitated was over 10,000. This was a big task.

A profile of the state VR agency's expenditures on facilities between 1969 and 1974 supports Adams' admitted goal of utilizing their services (Table 4.5).

As much as half (and in 1969 and 1974 over half) of Adams' total client services expenditures were used on facility services.

TABLE 4.5

Profile of Facility Expenditures

Year	State Facility Expendi- tures	Facility Expenditures as a Percentage of all Client Services Expenditures	National Rank of State Spent in Facilities	National Average Percentage Funds Spent in Facilities
1969	$4,117,165	54.0	2	24.0
1971	4,009,231	41.5	3	27.5
1972	4,498,723	43.4	2	28.0
1973	4,543,626	43.0	4	28.6
1974	5,848,486	55.4	3	30.9

Source: Federal vocational rehabilitation annual statistical profile, 1969-74.

FACILITY DIRECTORS' REACTION TO
ADAMS' POSITION, 1966-72

The External Influencers and Their
Means of Control

Mintzberg (1983) presented the concepts of external coalition and influencers, and internal coalition and influencers in describing power relations in and around organizations. Mintzberg discussed several means by which external influencers impinge on the internal coalition to impose and effect particular demands. Without going into detail or summarizing Mintzberg's many descriptive categories on this topic, we did find his notion of external influencers helpful. The facility directors' movement in our study could be regarded as external influencers on Adams' VR policy objectives. Mintzberg noted five kinds of direct controls external coalitions employ to exert influence on internal decision makers, which describe the facility directors' political influence on Adams. These controls include, "(1) accessing decision makers directly, (2) being included in an organizational decision-making process, (3) planting a representative in the Internal Coalition, (4) having the power to authorize one or more of the organization's decisions, and (5) actually imposing one or more of the organization's decisions on it directly" (1983:62). Facility directors attempted several of these controls before using the fifth one.

Adams' lack of an acceptable response to Gates' request for an explicit policy that would have enabled facilities to cover most of their operating costs for training severely handicapped clients led to an open split between the facility camp and Adams.

Gates took his case to the governor and to the state finance committee in the early 1970s. He successfully lobbied these committees to designate a two-year line-item specific percentage of Adams' budget, to be spent solely for rehabilitation facility services. Gates commented on this action:

> Almost all rehabilitation facilities joined in on the motion. We had no choice. Adams refused to listen to our needs. It was a real victory for us. We were part of the rehabilitation process; our role was important and we showed that. We weren't going to be pushed around.

This event marked a turning point in the relations between facility directors and the state VR agency. Since that incident, the adversarial element in the relationship between Adams and the metropolitans in particular became evident.

The consequences of the game between Adams and facility directors can, from our reconstruction of the evidence presented, be evaluated as follows.

The metropolitan directors we interviewed were largely dissatisfied with Adams' lack of policies toward their operations after 1966. He was viewed as a political figure who knew vocational rehabilitation but who, later in his term, became more engulfed in his own goals to gain successful rehabilitations than in helping clients or in assisting facilities to help clients.

Beyond their attitudes and opinions of Adams and his policies, Adams' budgets showed that facilities were substantially built up and used during his term. Fiscally and programmatically, then, facilities gained from Adams' administration.

In terms of gaining a foothold in Adams' critical decision-making activities between 1966 and 1974, with the exception of their success with the state legislature in 1972, facility directors were not successful.

The rural directors were satisfied with Adams' approach and with his support of their programs, with the exceptions of their coalition with the metropolitans in 1972. Administrators

indicated that they viewed him as interested in their daily
activities, helpful in getting them resources, and knowledgeable
about workshop operations and rehabilitation in general.

OUTCOMES OF ADAMS' PURSUIT FOR
ORGANIZATIONAL AUTONOMY

Adams' intended objective of gaining organizational and
administrative autonomy centered as much on his moving out
of the vocational education system as on moving to the newly
created Department of Health and Social Services (DHSS) in
the state. Adams' reasons for moving to DHSS were based on
his belief that he could more freely access state legislators,
relate to other human service provider agencies, and that he
could also gain more administrative autonomy to pursue political
program-building activities.

Our evidence indicates that Adams' move to DHSS provided
him in the short term (1967-70) with more opportunity and
authority to capture federal money to increase his staff and
his program budget. Had he remained as an adjunct program
with the vocational education system, he would have had to
continue submitting budget requests through the Board, which
viewed the VR program as a small and, at times, rival subsystem
of their service network.

As part of DHSS, Adams' program became an autonomous
division within a more loosely coupled system, at least at the
time Adams joined it. Figure 4.1 is an organizational chart of
DHSS, showing the position of the VR program in the larger
structure.

The secretary of the department was a tenured civil service
employee and friend of Adams. The secretary answered to the
governor. The secretary enjoyed considerable administrative
discretion and permitted divisional directors the same autonomy
in running their programs.

The newness of the agency and the secretary's laissez-
faire administrative style gave other divisional directors
considerable discretion and capacity to pursue their program
missions in a loosely coordinated way. The secretary's style
suited Adams' desire for more administrative independence to
network at the federal VR level.

Adams' salary significantly increased as a result of his
move to DHSS. He also became a tenured civil service state
employee. Moreover, his visibility and more independent
administrative status added to his prestige and influence among

FIGURE 4.1

DHSS Organizational Chart

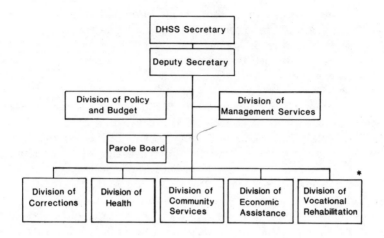

Source: VR Agency Documents in State Historical Archives.

other state human service directors, legislators, and regional and federal VR administrators. As Adams related to us:

> I dropped the title Assistant State Director of Voca-
> tional and Adult Education for Vocational Rehabilita-
> tion. Fred saw our program getting bigger than
> vocational education. When I went to the Department
> of Social Services, he saw I was serious about making
> things happen. I was able to deal my own hand with
> the legislators.

While Adams' move to DHSS enabled him to respond more directly to obtaining state matching funds, changes within DHSS in the early 1970s set in motion events that later constrained the autonomy Adams had enjoyed within that structure. First, the governor initiated and won legislative changes that brought DHSS directly under his control. After the retirement of the first DHSS secretary (Adams' friend), the governor received power to appoint his successors. Second, all divisional directors in DHSS became appointees of the governor. In effect, DHSS became a more politicized body in the 1970s. Adams experienced

the effects of these changes with the governor's appointment
of a new DHSS secretary. Adams commented to us,

> The new guy was a flat tire. He was an Eastern
> lawyer brought in to reorganize everything.
> Planners and managers were supposed to tell us
> how to run our program, but first they tried to
> get us to educate them on what we were doing.
> It was a mess. Too much red tape.

Third, centralization increased at DHSS. The second DHSS
secretary attempted to centralize the divisional structure of
DHSS by delegating more authority to the Divisions of Management Services and Policy and Budget (see the DHSS organization
chart, Fig. 4.1). More fiscal reports and meetings were demanded
of the divisional directors. The watchdog activities of these
two divisions changed the organizational emphasis of DHSS
from a loosely coupled system to a large-scale machine bureaucracy (Mintzberg 1983) dominated by a top-down administrative
control system.

From 1970 forward, the focus of the VR staff's communication exchanges changed dramatically. Until this time, memos,
letters, and recorded meetings centered on field activities.
From the late 1960s and especially into the 1970s, the bulk of
the written communications by Adams and his central office
staff were directed to DHSS Management and Policy and Budget
personnel. The topics covered issues relating to compliance
standards, reorganization ideas, program evaluation, and
budget information. Adams commented to us on these changes:

> I had to hire staff to shuffle papers, play with
> statistics and go to meetings. A lot of our time
> was spent telling department planners what we
> were doing so they could tell us not to do it.

These organizational changes constrained but did not pre-
vent or hinder Adams from aggressively capturing available
federal VR funds until his retirement, as his budget expenditures
showed.

RESULTANT STRATEGIES: ADAMS' LOGICS OF
ACTION, LA ACCOMMODATION, COMPETITION,
PRESTIGE, POWER, AND COERCION

Adams implemented his major strategic choices during this
period based on the logics of accommodation, competition, prestige,

power, and coercion. While these logics overlapped in many of Adams' decisions, we have reconstructed our observations based on the events outlined earlier.

LA Accommodation

Adams initially adopted a logic of action based on accommodation to pursue his expansionist aims. He was constrained by restrictive federal regulations from obtaining funds to enlarge his program. He discovered that by accommodating other power ful individuals and groups he could use their influence to access the federal political, legislative, and fiscal VR system. He was also constrained by the vocational education board director's conservative fiscal and program policies toward the VR domain. Adams described the director's attitudes toward the VR program as jealous, noncommittal, and uninformed. Because the VR program was an adjunct part of the vocational education system, Adams sought accommodative relationships with other powerful groups in attempts to leverage the Board's VR-related policies.

Adams responded to the external constraints of his limited access to federal and state VR funds by coalescing and bargaining with facility directors and the noted Congressman Lands. Facility directors needed federal funds to expand their physical plants and programs; Adams needed facility grassroots support to leverage state legislators' and the Board director's VR funding decisions. Adams interested Congressman Lands in the VR network, which represented a powerful local, state, and national voting constituency. Over a four-year period Adams was able through Lands to change the federal funding matching requirement in favor of facilities demands. Adams consequently won the support and alliance of facility groups, who, in turn, provided him with additional grassroots leverage over state legislators' funding decisions.

Adams sought federal money to expand his program through available but competitive grants. Our observations showed that, again, through bargaining with Lands and influential state university professors, Adams was able to access funds to innovate and expand his program.

We observed that Lands agreed to help Adams obtain federal grant funds if a particular $5 million innovative project was located in his district in the state. The university professors agreed to write and monitor the grant since they would be provided with additional staff and research. Adams gained in this effort by strengthening his relationship with Lands, expanding his program, and by receiving recognition in the state as an innovator.

LA Competition and Prestige: Adams' Strategic
Logic and Responses to the Great Society
Growth Trends, 1966-74

Between 1966 and 1974 Adams altered his accommodative
logic to one based on competition and prestige. He did so for
three reasons. First, he and his staff perceived metropolitan
facility directors as threatening to take control of VR client
policy. Second, Adams' program achievements through 1967
led him to seek more national recognition and prestige. Third,
the abundance of federal funds for VR programs enhanced
Adams' already competitive desire to extend his program and
political turf.

Adams, then, set out not merely to expand his program
in the late 1960s, but to build an empire by competing nationally
with other states and with the metropolitans in this state. By
the end of the decade in fact, he was well known in national
VR circles. He had also, as we showed earlier, ranked in the
top ten among all states for the highest number of client rehabilitations obtained.

LA Power: Adams' Structuring and Control
of the Internal Organization

We posited three hypothetical relationships at the outset
of this chapter:

H-1c. Administrators who originate or change their organizational structures by elaboration and diversification,
increase the likelihood of successfully implementing
expansionist strategies within a growth environment.
H-1d. The dominant organizational processes administrators
will use to increase the likelihood of enlarging their
domains in growth environments are field-related operations combined with planning activities.
H-1e. Administrators who, during growth periods, select and
implement a dominant internal control strategy of
innovation/promotion increase the likelihood of motivating
their staff to implement expansionist objectives and
strategies.

Evidence from previous sections validated the first hypothesis (H-1c). The second hypothesis (H-1d) we found to have
been partially accurate. Adams did emphasize and concentrate
most of his energy on bolstering field and counseling functions

in the program. However, he deemphasized the much needed
long-term planning element in favor of a political, personal,
and autocratic decision-making style. For example, Adams'
planning and budget administrator informed us,

> Adams was a power broker. He formed unholy
> alliances to get more power. He was not the darling
> of the governor, but he had made enough influen-
> tial contacts with national figures that he didn't
> need all the state connections he once wanted.
> Politics and power were his main concerns. He
> used the agency and other relations as instru-
> ments to polish his own image and status nationally.
> Adams was numero uno, and that meant using any
> and everybody he could to get his way. He didn't
> give a damn, really, about planning or running
> the program from quality standards. His goal
> was to get the highest percentage of 26s [success-
> ful rehabilitations] in the nation.

Finally, we hypothesized (H-1e) that an internal administrative control strategy based on innovation/promotion would
motivate staff to successfully implement expansionist objectives.
Again, we found this partially to have been the case. Adams
successfully appealed to field staff to carry out his competitive
and expansionist strategies based on an ideology (Downs 1967:
237) or loyalty to the mission of the program.

With his top-level management staff, however, he used
the logics of power and coercion to control internal communications, input, and work activities. For example, the chief
planning administrator reflected common themes in our interviews
with the central office staff:

> Adams was a dictator. All major decisions were
> his. Anybody who didn't go along with him found
> themselves isolated from him. We used to call the
> game he played with us, "Who's in the garbage
> can?" Every other week Adams stopped speaking
> to someone for something they said or did. When
> we found out who that was, we stopped communi-
> cating with him so Adams could see we were on
> his side.

Adams, then, used his personal, charismatic power to
persuade field staff to identify with an ideology (Downs 1967)
based on the theme the client is our mission. Adams used his

position power and simple, coercive control techniques (Edwards 1977) to align top-level management staff to his strategies.

UNINTENDED CONSEQUENCES OF ADAMS' STRATEGIC RESPONSES TO THE GROWTH ENVIRONMENT

Adams, without intending it, helped institutionalize the independent role and strategic importance of private rehabilitation facilities in the VR process in his state and nationally. While our evidence indicated that he deliberately used facilities to achieve his expansionist ends, he did not foresee that his achievements through the Lands Amendment and through his efforts to build and enhance facility usage would result in their gaining a predominant role, apart from his desired use of them, as major participants in the VR client service arena.

Adams had also unintentionally institutionalized a set of expectations from facility directors and other service providers in the state regarding his style of negotiating funds and programs, and of resolving conflicts. Specifically, his style involved a face-to-face approach.

Our interviews with facility directors who had worked with Adams indicated they enjoyed communicating with him. Folktales, legends, and gossip related to rehab provided a common basis for their communications. Adams' successors were from other professional fields. Expectations of facility directors to communicate with later VR administrators on a similar informal and frequent basis would be violated.

Organizationally, by merging with DHSS Adams had (unknowingly at the time) placed his organization within what became a rigid, centralized, bureaucratic structure—one that became a partial instrument of the governor. Moreover, Adams' own organizational emphasis on direct client services was later constrained by DHSS reporting and reorganizing demands.

Also, by enlarging his staff to accommodate the growth demands in federal VR legislation, Adams incorporated well-educated, professional, central office management administrators who found his simple and personal charismatic leadership style arbitrary, autocratic, and more politically motivated than program oriented. Serious conflicts resulted between Adams and several of his planners.

Finally, as a combined result of Adams' programmatic emphasis on quantitative measures of field staff performance, and his informal, lax control techniques with field supervisors, an alleged scandal was reported in the program. In December 1973, an informant in the state wrote a letter to the state Department of Administration alleging that two vocational rehabilitation field office staff were using funds for their personal use:

> Apparently, with the consent of the district super-
> visors they [VR staff] are writing authorizations
> and state purchase orders for merchandise using
> a client's number but keeping the merchandise for
> themselves. For example, it is believed that the
> Hanson VR District Office outfitted their entire
> office with softball uniforms using state funds.
> Many other items have been bought this way includ-
> ing at least two snowmobiles for personal use. . . .
> in one instance $100 dollars worth of walnut lumber
> was purchased by the Hanson VR office and given
> to the State Administrator of the Division. . . .
> While you may accept or reject this information, a
> cursory investigation by your department would
> undoubtedly reveal widespread fraud and mismanage-
> ment.

The State Department of Administration made arrangements to have an audit of the VR offices listed in the informant's letter. The Legislative Audit Bureau sent a team of auditors to initiate the review.

In response to the audit Adams wrote the chairperson of the State Joint Committee on Legislative Organization, on October 29, 1974:

> While the Division welcomes the opportunity for an
> appropriate program audit, the net result of the
> auditors' activities to date has been an almost total
> disruption of the work of the Hanson District. An
> atmosphere of suspicion and confusion has developed
> with a resulting lowering of staff morale and
> effectiveness. . . . Overall, their approach to our
> staff, clients, and vendors was perceived as being
> treated and related to as a criminal with extreme
> and persistent displays of arrogance. . . . I am
> shocked and dismayed to think our state accepts
> and endorses these tactics and procedures in the
> name of program reviewer. . . .

The Legislative Audit Bureau's report was issued on December 20, 1974. The basic findings of the report were sent to the governor. Essentially, the major findings and recommendations were as follows:

Our examination of the Division of Vocational Rehabilitation's Hanson District Office operations disclosed that the office is seriously mismanaged and has not achieved the results concerning "rehabilitated" clients as reported to the legislature, executive office, and the Health and Social Services Board. We are recommending that the Department of Health and Social Services:

—Replace the Hanson District Office supervisor and review the duties, responsibilities and performance of the rest of the district staff. . . .
—Immediately install meaningful financial and program internal controls. Existing controls are extremely weak which adversely affected the program. . . .

Audit findings concerning a possible misuse of funds at Hanson were also discussed with the DHSS secretary. Based on our findings, the secretary requested the State Department of Justice to make a formal investigation.

This investigation has resulted in John Doe hearings currently in progress. For this reason, our audit findings concerning possible misuse of funds are not discussed in this report.

Other findings in the audit showed that a large number of rehabilitated were clients discovered not to have been successfully rehabilitated. The Hanson District Office supervisor was demoted and removed from that position.

PRELIMINARY HYPOTHESES READDRESSED

We began our inquiry with the following hypothesis:

Administrative leaders who can successfully select and implement expansionist objectives and strategies in an external environment characterized by growth increase the likelihood of enlarging their organizational domain and control over resources.

Our findings indicated that Adams was successful in strategically selecting and accessing external resources through political means, but that he was unsuccessful in effectively integrating these resources into his operating organization. Conflicts emerged between Adams and his top management staff as well as with facility directors.

Lack of effective internal management controls combined with an exaggerated emphasis on quantitative performance standards contributed to scandal in the program. Adams' failure at effective internal administration was, we found, largely a result of his preoccupation with the external political aspects of strategy formation.

Our findings concur with Katz and Kahn's (1978) assertion that charismatic leadership style is effective in providing a wide perspective on the environment. Certainly, Adams' charisma, which was rooted in his career experience and understanding of the program, was instrumental in his obtaining access to powerful people and resources to expand his program. However, while his charisma enhanced his boundary-spanning and external negotiating activities, his zealousness inhibited him from delegating authority inside the organization and integrating the expertise he needed to successfully run the organization.

Our results also indicate that Adams initially used a logic of action based on accommodation to implement his expansionist objectives. With facility directors, in particular, he negotiated his interests between 1961 and 1965 through cooperative means. Changes in the external environment, Adams' objectives, and facility directors' demands all led to Adams' adoption of a competitive external negotiation logic and tactics. While this logic and related tactics did not impede Adams' ability to obtain federal funding for his program, it did constrain both his relationship with metropolitan facility directors and his freedom to later control the distribution of funds to the field (since the facility directors helped legislate demands on his budget to their advantage).

Based on our observations presented earlier, we argued that Adams overextended his organizational staff during the growth period to accommodate federal legislative mandates and to satisfy his competitive logic, which resulted in empire-building activities.

Although he also diversified his staffing activities by adding new expertise and by enlarging job responsibilities, he did so without assigning authority based on expertise. Most of his staff, according to our interviews, felt they performed their duties strictly according to Adams' arbitrary and competitive performance program demands placed on them.

As shown earlier, Adams succeeded more in motivating field staff to implement his strategies than he did in gaining the compliance of top-level management staff. We concluded that Adams effectively used an ideology and control tactic based on identification to gain the compliance of field staff. But he ineffectively used a simple, personal, and arbitrary control tactic based on coercion to discipline top management staff to conform to his political program objectives.

These observations suggest that a close examination of a charismatic leadership style and strategies that stem from an expansionist perspective bear certain costs.

In such a qualitative style as this, it is important to show that other explanations exist to view descriptions of events differently. While we argue our findings, we suggest that others could rival these with at least their alternative views.

ALTERNATIVE EXPLANATIONS OF ADAMS' STRATEGIC ACTIVITIES

Two explanations of Adams' choices that rival the inter-pretations in this chapter can be identified. The first is the rehabilitation facility perspective; the second is the transmission belt perspective.

Rehabilitation Facility Perspective

According to Gates and the other two directors of Seaside's large rehabilitation facilities, Adams had no choice but to use their plants and services during this period. Excerpts from our interviews with these three directors exemplify this perspec-tive:

Gates: Adams had no choice but to use facilities. He needed facilities to do his work; he had to play ball with us. Look, Arco [name of Gates' facility] had the first facility contract with DVR [Division of Vocational Rehabilitation]. DVR never used any other facility between 1955 and 1962. We had the first mentally retarded programs in the state. When the flood gates of federal legislation opened in the 1960s, Adams had no one else to turn to to take all the mentally ill and the emotionally disturbed.

Simmons: We had the training equipment and the space to handle large numbers of really severely disabled people. Vocational technical schools were too advanced for these clients.

Randolph: Voc Rehab counselors used us because they didn't have other options for many clients. Instead of sending a client back home, he could be placed in our facility for evaluation, training, or in a lot of instances just to have a more constructive place to gain a sense of self-worth.

We contend that Adams did need rehabilitation facilities. However, he needed them more from his own expansionist objectives and strategies than because of external pressures. As a noted professor of behavioral disabilities at the state university who worked with Adams stated:

> In my opinion, Adams' biggest mistake was to rely on the services of private facilities in the state. He could have built and run state-operated facilities like so many other states did. He created more dependence on their costly operations than was necessary.

Another explanation that counters the argument that Adams had no other choice except to use facilities is one given by the then director of the vocational education board:

> He [Adams] didn't have to break away from the Vocational Education program. He made the move to help himself and facilities, in that order. Vocational rehabilitation is more related to vocational and technical education services than to facility work. But Adams changed the emphasis of the rehabilitation program toward facilities. It was politics and power.

The Transmission Belt Perspective

This view, as noted by McLanahan (1979:3), "assumes that public programs contain well-defined goals which are made by Congress and implemented by an administrative apparatus that is structured along the lines of the classical Weberian bureaucracy." McLanahan also quotes Stewart (1975:1675) on this perspective, stating that the traditional model of administrative law "conceives of the agency as a mere transmission belt for implementing legislative directives in particular cases."

From this view, Adams as administrator of the state VR program had no choice but to administer federal funds and legislation at the state level. Discretion has no place in this perspective. As one facility director noted about this period in which Adams served, federal money ran like water. King Kong could have done the job of administrator and accomplished the same results.

The evidence presented in this chapter contradicts the transmission belt perspective. First, had Adams kept VR as an adjunct program in the vocational education system, it is questionable whether he could have obtained the sizable federal VR funds that he did. Second, there is evidence that other states within the same federal designated VR region as this did not obtain the same level of expansion in their programs as Adams. Prohibitive circumstances such as the following blocked growth in other states.

Many VR programs were constrained as subsystems in departments of labor, education, and welfare, and other such state governmental arrangements. Adams succeeded through coalitional and individual efforts to separate his program from an organizational situation that would constrain him.

Federal VR funds were available only on a state legislative matching basis. Those VR administrators who could not wield sufficient political influence to obtain matching funds could not—and did not—greatly expand their programs during this period. Even though the economic and political climate of this state was conducive during most of this period to furthering social service programs, considerable administrative effort was required to access the system.

CONCLUSION

In effect, the charismatic Adams left office having greatly expanded his staff and program, although conflicts between groups and individuals existed throughout the organization. He also obtained autonomy for his structure, but it was an autonomy constrained under a newer bureaucratic umbrella agency in the state. Scandal finally hit the program as a result of Adams' overconfidence and lenience with his field staff. Workshop facility directors around the state were mixed in their remembrances of Adams and his policies. Rural directors revered him; metropolitans respected but distrusted him.

Adams took on a significant mission and set of tasks for himself. He achieved most of his aims but with costs he had not anticipated. As Anthony Downs noted, zealots "antagonize other officials by their refusal to be impartial and their willingness to trample all obstacles" (1967:110).

NOTES

1. The term domain was used by Miles (1982) to describe an organization's strategic adaptation patterns to external events. We use the term to denote Adams' intentional objectives and strategies that guided his responses to federal legislative and economic changes.

2. It should be noted that part of the bargain between Adams and Baird was that the project be located in Baird's district. It was. After two years of operation, the county welfare director in the county in which the project was located publicly recognized the program's value. In a letter to Congressman Baird dated May 15, 1967, the welfare director stated, "As far as the relief load in _____ County is concerned, it has been more than cut in half since the inception of the project. Just prior to the beginning of the project, the relief load totaled 145 cases. On May 1, 1967, it totaled 59 cases."

3. While there were other players in this game, we focus mainly on Adams and facility directors since the interactions between these two parties were linked to commonly sought resources, namely, federal funds, clients, and power to control policy that regulated clients. The specific objectives and strategies of the two parties differed but the resources they desired were basically the same.

4. The total expenditures of these years are accurate. However, members of Adams' top management staff claimed administrative salaries were hidden in the program and client-related expenditures.

5

Administrative Strategies during the Critically Turbulent Period

How do administrators who succeed charismatic zealots in organizations manage operations in an increasingly turbulent environment with the same staff and diminished resources? This chapter focuses on this question and the responses of the second VR administrator, Brown, to the turbulent events between 1975 and 1978. While Brown's term was significantly shorter than Adams', Brown is important to this study in that he had the responsibility of realigning the organization to meet external demands different from those Adams had faced; and Brown had to do so with most of Adams' former staff.[1] Moreover, as the first administrator appointed outside the VR and vocational educational systems, Brown had to orient staff to his new role and strategies. The extent to which he succeeded in accomplishing these tasks, the methods he used, and the associated organizational costs are dealt with here. A set of preliminary hypotheses was developed from management literature to structure these observations.

PRELIMINARY HYPOTHESES

The hypotheses for this chapter are based on works by Jauch and Osborn (1981) and Thain (1976). Jauch and Osborn developed predictive strategic profiles and goal orientations that top management can use to align strategies with environmental context and organizational structure. Two of their four strategic profiles are referred to in this chapter and are briefly discussed.

Under one strategic profile, the environment is character-ized as uncertain. In this situation, Jauch and Osborn argue for a diversified organizational structure and flexible strategies. In another strategic profile these authors characterize an en-vironment that is in flux and developing. A structure that is organic and a goal orientation that emphasizes a product/service orientation is required.

They argue that when the environment is complicated and uncertain,

> One can also look at a profile of [strategic] predis-positions consistent with an emphasis on technical leadership (product/service quality). Here the environmental focus is likely to be on competitors; the environment may be seen in an unfavorable light. . . . A technical leadership orientation is likely to correlate with a formalized vertical struc-ture and a stress on controls such as MBO. One could also expect budgetary review based on interim financial plans. (p. 494)

Another organizational theorist, Thain (1976), presented a sequence of stages in an organization's development. He characterized three stages, two of which are relevant to this period in the study. Stage I (the one-person show) character-ized, to a large extent, the period and activities of Adams: major strategic issues concentrated on growth-related problems; personal and subjective goals were used; strategies centered on exploitation of immediate opportunities; control was based on subjective, simple systems, using communication and observa-tion; major organizational emphases were placed on operating orientations as opposed to a product or functional emphasis. Stage II, similar in characteristics to the period examined here, is a transition from the first stage. This stage emphasizes a strategic orientation based on more sophisticated control and accounting systems to respond to an environment characterized as more complex. More structure, formal policies, and specializa-tion are needed in this stage to deal with environmental complex-ity.

While these sources are based on private sector organiza-tions, we found the underlying logic applicable to the public sector agency in this study.

Based on the arguments presented in the above stated sources, the following hypothetical statements were used as a basis to guide our observations of Brown's strategic activities:

H-3.   Administrative leaders who can successfully select and
       implement production-related objectives and strategies
       in an external environment characterized by critical
       turbulence increase the likelihood of protecting and
       promoting their desired organizational domain.

H-3a. A leadership style that is technically competent during
       critically turbulent periods will enable administrators to
       select and successfully implement and emphasize produc-
       tion objectives and strategies.

H-3b. Major external negotiation tactics of legitimating and
       emphasizing productivity will increase the likelihood of
       administrators' protecting their desired organizational
       domain during critically turbulent periods.

H-3c. Administrators who originate or change their organiza-
       tional structure by decentralizing and diversifying
       decision making increase the likelihood of implementing
       production objectives and strategies during a critically
       turbulent period.

H-3d. The dominant organizational processes administrators
       will use to increase the likelihood of protecting their
       domain is measurement, control, and production.

H-3e. Administrators who, during critically turbulent periods,
       select and implement a dominant internal control strategy
       of accountability increase the likelihood of motivating
       their staff to implement production-related objectives.

The turbulent events and external context that affected
Brown's strategic orientation during this period are explained
next. Evidence identifying Brown's intended strategic responses
are then presented, along with plans to manage the turbulence.

TURBULENT EVENTS AND TRENDS, 1975-78

The specific events and trends described here created a
critically turbulent policymaking environment for Brown at this
state level in the following ways. First, at risk for the VR
program was a loss of legitimacy by other organizations. Benson
(1975) noted the significance of legitimacy as an organizational
resource. Combined federal and state legislative investigations
and reports that revealed mismanagement and scandal in this
and other state programs raised the question of the VR administrator's ability to carry out the program's legislated mandates.
Second, the extent of the state's organizational vulnerability

was heightened because of the tremendous turbulent pressures exerted on the agency both within its boundaries (from DHSS demands) and from outside (state legislative audit, declining state economy, and coalitional activities of workshops).

Levine (1978) also noted the following factors, which contribute to an organization's vulnerability: small size, internal conflict, changes in leadership, lack of a base of expertise, and absence of a positive self-image. In the case of this state's VR program, the major contributing factors to the agency's vulnerability included pressures in the federal and state environment, effects of a change from a charismatic to a politically accountable leadership style; and, related to the second factor, the lack of procedural and policy consistency in the transition of administrators. Turbulence in the environment is described at the national, state, and local levels.

The National Level

National trends and events in the VR policy arena between 1974 and 1978 can be characterized as politically turbulent and congressionally restrictive. In particular, the 1973 federal regulations, which required state agencies to serve more severely handicapped clients, were implemented in full force two years after passage. The effects of these regulations on this and other state VR agencies created confusion among VR counselors over the definition of severely handicapped clients, strained VR counselors' case service funds to serve severely handicapped clients, and added conflict between administrative goals that required quantitative (the number of clients who obtained employment) and qualitative (the very severely disabled clients could live independently) indicators of success.

Also at the national level, there was a general congressional mood after Watergate that stressed overcautiousness and accountability. Wright (1980:152) characterized that national climate as follows:

> The 93rd Congress asserted power in terms of increased specificity in the provisions of laws affecting handicapped people. Distrustful of the Nixon Administration's commitment to social programs generally, and programs for handicapped people in particular, congressional committees tended to include detailed statutory specifications regarding the operation of federal programs.

Congress for the first time involved the GAO (General Accounting Office) in the area of programs for the disabled. Congress also established deadlines for submittal of regulations and requirements relating to performance standards in VR state programs. These actions, taken together, demonstrated a national climate of congressional restlessness and reaction in the wake of Watergate.

Turbulence at the State and Local Levels

At the state level a number of events and trends reflected a climate similar to that described at the national level. Specifically, the state legislative audit bureau's (LAB) investigation over the mismanagement of VR funds and fraudulent reporting practices during Adams' term continued to affect the agency's operations. The Department of Health and Social Services was, for example, pressured by state legislators to take a more active regulatory role in the VR program's affairs.

Additionally, evidence from national studies on other state VR agencies' mismanagement practices increased the watchdog functions of regional VR offices on state programs. An excerpt from a 1979 article written in the Journal of Applied Rehabilitation Counseling exemplified this point:

A series of studies conducted from 1969 to 1975 by the General Accounting Office, the Department of Health, Education, and Welfare Audit Agency, and the Rehabilitation Services Administration indicate that problems in the public rehabilitation program exist and that they have been recurring in nature. These problems have been identified as the provision of insubstantial services; poor case documentation; inadequate benefits obtained by clients; large numbers of clients who are not gainfully employed; the provision of services to ineligible clients; and the failure of the Social Security Disability Insurance Program to remain cost effective. The state-federal program throughout this period initiated training programs in job placement, supervisory training, case recording and documentation; yet, the problems persisted. Confronted with these evaluations and implied criticisms, the State-Federal Program of Vocational Rehabilitation began to institute measures to correct these deficiencies. Many

of these measures established additional requirements of a controlling nature. (p. 81)

Another turbulent influence on VR activities in this state
was the reorganization plans of the agency (DHSS) that housed
the VR program. The new DHSS secretary planned to consolidate
all divisions into operating substructures of his umbrella agency.
Key staff positions in all divisions within DHSS were recalled
to serve in a centralized capacity at the departmental level.
Personnel, fiscal, and computer programming positions were
to be taken from Brown's staff and other divisions and integrated
under the control of the new department secretary. This plan
caused considerable problems for Brown.

The governor also imposed an austerity program on spending by state agencies. This program was identified in a memorandum from the DHSS secretary to all division administrators.
An excerpt from the memorandum dated December 6, 1974, is
quoted as saying:

> On November 29, 1974, Governor Lewins advised
> all state agencies that this state was facing an
> uncertain fiscal future, and that restraints on
> spending must be immediately initiated by state
> government. All departments have been directed
> to make a tough and careful self-analysis of
> expenditure requirements, cutting costs wherever
> possible.

Obtaining state matching funds would become problematic for
Brown with this funding restriction.

State legislation passed in 1971 and 1972 also complicated
Brown's administration. These laws created county boards to
staff programs designated to serve very severely mentally and
emotionally ill persons. By 1975 these boards were well established and entrenched in the state. Another competitive set
of players was, in effect, added to the rehabilitation game.

By 1974 private rehabilitation facility directors in the
state were also better organized. Two powerful and influential
formal organizations now existed, the RFA (Rehabilitation
Facility Directors Association), which included statewide
membership, and the Council of Seaside Association, which
included Gates (from Chapter 4) and other powerful urban
directors.

Facility directors continued to pressure Adams' successor
for a share in the control of VR policy and funding. During

this period, they attempted to use the DHSS secretary and other county board directors to pressure Brown for VR funds. The key players in the game expanded to include the DHSS director, county board directors, and to a lesser extent, vocational educational system personnel.

BROWN'S BACKGROUND, LEADERSHIP STYLE, AND SELECTION

Earlier we posited that

A leadership style that is technically competent during critically turbulent periods will enable administrators to select and successfully implement and emphasize production objectives and strategies.

In this section we characterize Brown's style through interviews with him, his staff, and others who knew him.

Brown's Leadership Style: Political Strategist

Wright (1980:165) noted that

A trend in the 1970s was for some governors to appoint business administrators, politicians, or severely disabled persons who had neither the agency experience nor the professional preparation needed to head a state rehabilitation agency.

Brown was an example of this trend. He was an outsider to the VR group in the state. Brown, for example, told us in an interview,

When I entered this program, I was already down on three counts: I didn't have a degree in rehabilitation; I didn't have an advanced degree; and I was a politician. The jargon people in the agency used was "foreign." Rehabilitation was like a religion to them. They didn't just work in the program, they believed in it, talked it, lived it.

I started the job by learning the budget and the field operations. Once I had learned the funda-

mentals of these operations, I knew I could assert
my influence and bring change. I brought a sense
of power and political awareness to the job. I knew
the broader political context of the state, not one
perspective. I gained respect in the agency because
of my background and direct approach to solving
problems, and there were enough problems at the
time.

Based on our interviews with his top management staff,
we reconstructed Brown's style as a political strategist during
these years. His leadership characteristics based on these
interviews are summarized as follows: First, Brown brought a
political problem-solving perspective to the agency. He read
the environment in terms of actors and interest groups with
demands that either threatened or supported his agency goals.
Excerpts from our interviews with two of Brown's top-level
administrators exemplify this observation:

First Administrator: Brown was a politician first and then an
administrator. I gave him credit for his ability to work the
system. He helped the agency by negotiating our budget
with the politicians. He found out everything he could
about anybody who might get in his way. A lot of field
staff didn't agree with him because he could change directions
fast without telling those who had to do the changing.
Second Administrator: He taught us how to think politically.
Before, we used to act like the program was the center of
everything. When Brown came, we learned to analyze
everyone's motives, gains and losses before we implemented
a plan. Brown used to say, "There's more square feet of
idealism among this staff than in the entire state government." He changed that. When he asked for reports and
information from staff, they had to defend and justify their
views. One staffer said he felt like we were playing war
games in the agency with Brown as the commander. Adams
used to make a decision, tell us about it and we'd do it.
Brown would feel us out for information about different
options and people who were involved. He found out as
much about us as the information he wanted.

Second, Brown used his legislative and political contacts
to enhance the agency's budget position in the state during
this period. An excerpt from our interview with the agency's
management services administrator exemplified this point:

> When Brown came on board, we had a legislated
> line-item in our Budget from facilities that required
> us to buy a percentage of their services. He was
> with us less than a year before he got that removed.
> He did more on the phone for us with the legislature
> than most department [DHSS] administrators could
> do in months.

Other members of Brown's management staff supported the
observation that Brown's influence with state legislators was
substantial.

Third, Brown used selected top-level staff members to
educate and advise him on critical organizational and staffing
issues. Although he made all final decisions, he used input
from selected staff to formulate options.

Unlike Adams, our evidence indicated that Brown did not
perceive his role with DVR in historical, vocationally related
institutional terms. He saw himself, as did his staff, as a
trouble-shooter and strategic problem-solver rather than a
statesman. And although (also unlike Adams) he lacked technical program and administrative knowledge and experience, he
had an impressive range of political skills as a former legislator.

Brown's Background and Selection

Based on interviews with Brown and with individuals who
worked for the governor and the DHSS secretary at that time,
we determined that Brown was selected to administer the VR
agency during this critical period for two reasons. He had
established sufficient political clout in the state legislature.
He had proven to the governor and to the new DHSS secretary
that he could restore legitimacy to this agency. Following the
investigation and published findings from the 1974 audit, the
state rehabilitation program became a target for certain powerful
legislators to attack the governor and the DHSS bureaucracy.
Scandal in any public bureaucracy provides such a political
opportunity.

Brown seemed the logical answer to help the governor in
this continuing problem, since he had been the state's youngest
Senate Democratic majority leader. He had held that post when
he was in his twenties. He had also served on several important
legislative committees and was familiar with the legislative
budgeting and political process.

Brown recounted this view of his selection in an excerpt
from one of our interviews:

The governor called me to the mansion to meet the
new DHSS secretary. He was an easterner and was
chosen to take charge of the department to get it
reorganized. They both knew that it had been in
trouble since the 1974 legislative audit and they
wanted someone who would get that division in order,
especially with the legislature. I had contacts and
friends in the legislature since I had worked there.
They believed my contacts and background could
assist the new secretary in his reorganization
efforts as well. I gave it some thought and later
accepted.

The second reason Brown was appointed to this post was
his desire and need for a high-level government post to help
him move from a political to an administrative career. He told
us in an interview,

I wanted a challenge and was getting tired of the
work in the legislature. I had achieved what I
wanted there and thought this would be educational
and a good experience. I thought I could also find
out if I liked that type of work.

Because of his youth and quick, successful rise to political
power in the state, Brown's administrative experience was minimal. He had served only as an assistant to a hospital administrator in the northern part of the state where he had lived.
While he was skilled in manipulating people and budgets, he
had no experience or education in federal administration or
vocational rehabilitation at the time he took this position.
    Brown, then, came to the agency for career advancement
motives and to assist the governor with a political and organizational challenge which, if accomplished, could have advanced
his administrative credibility and political standing in state
governmental circles.
    Brown's leadership style differed from that of Adams in
that Brown was motivated by political interests, not programmatic
ones. While both Brown and Adams were skilled strategists,
Brown's intention was to promote the program for political gain.
Adams identified with the program. Brown was also concerned
with changing policy rather than creating it. Whereas Adams'
strategic objectives focused on global domain activities, Brown
emphasized short-term operational directives. Brown's task
was to manage changing external events that he neither created
nor understood well at the outset.

In the next section we explain Brown's intentions and methods of controlling the turbulence he inherited.

BROWN'S INTENDED AND ATTEMPTED STRATEGIC RESPONSES TO TURBULENT EVENTS

We posited at the outset that

Administrative leaders who can successfully select and implement production-related objectives and strategies in an external environment characterized by critical turbulence increase the likelihood of protecting and promoting their desired organizational domain.

Based on our interviews with Brown, and having examined his agency correspondence during this period, we found this hypothesis relevant but limited regarding the nature of his intended program objectives. Specifically, we argue in this section that while Brown emphasized policy directives based on productivity, he also focused his efforts on legitimating and fitting the agency with the structure and reorganization goals of the DHSS secretary.

Table 5.1 summarizes our reconstruction of Brown's intended dominant objectives and related strategies for the program he took over in the mid-1970s.

Legitimize DVR at the State Governmental Level

Brown pursued the objective of legitimizing the agency through a dominant strategy of aligning DVR closer to DHSS and that secretary's reorganization plan. The plan was sponsored by the governor as an attempt to coordinate activities of the expanding social service agencies in the state, which were duplicating costly and, in many cases, inefficient programs. Essentially, the plan divided the state into six areas. Certain divisional administrators in DHSS, including DVR, were requested to match their regions to these areas. The DHSS secretary's intent of regionalizing the state was to develop common areas in which different service providers could coordinate activities.

The plan also recommended that divisions that offered services to local areas should add staff called "regional administrators" to serve as links between their state offices and field locations. The intent was to decentralize the decision-making process and share information between central and field offices.

TABLE 5.1

Brown's Intended Strategic Responses to Turbulent Events

Intended Objectives	Related Strategies
1. Restore DVR's legitimacy at the state government level	1. Align DVR structure with DHSS reorganization plan 1.1 Implement innovative organizational project
2. Implement 1973 federal legislation	2. Increase staff productivity 2.1 Formalize and monitor productivity standards
3. Develop cooperative cost-control relationships with facilities and county program boards	3. Establish uniform cost allocation system with facilities 3.1 Develop closer working relationships with county boards

Source: Compiled by the author.

To ensure the coordination of statewide services, the DHSS secretary also recommended that each divisional administrator review position descriptions, budget reporting systems, and costs of operating the programs with the intent of structuring their organizations closer to the DHSS administration. Certain functions in each division were also planned to be centralized at a higher level in DHSS.

Brown began to orient his staff to implement organization-wide changes based on DHSS initiatives.

Brown's Restructuring of DVR

We stated above that

Administrators who originate or change their organizational structures by decentralizing and by diversifying decision making increase the likelihood of implementing production objectives and strategies during a critically turbulent period.

We also posited that

The dominant organizational processes administrators will use to increase the likelihood of protecting their domain are measurement, control, and production.

We found, however, that Brown intended to centralize critical decisions relating to field services at the central office level. He staffed six regional administrators under his control with the intention of having them carry out his directives in the field. As he stated in an interview,

> I knew that adding six more supervisors in the
> organization wouldn't make a lot of people happy,
> but I thought if I could use them to wake staff up
> who weren't working, why not? I didn't want to
> send out more higher paid people to have to disci-
> pline, so I made it clear to them who they were
> reporting to and why.

Although the DHSS secretary intended to use the regional administrators to enhance communication between local and central offices, Brown also tried to use these positions to monitor field staff performance activities and to enact his policy directives in the field. Brown's intended use of the regional administrators was based as much on control of field staff activities as on production objectives.

Brown also emphasized organizational processes aimed at legitimating the agency through statistical performance measures. He was not as concerned with protecting the program's domain as he was with controlling and legitimating the status of the program. We base these observations on our interviews with Brown, his deputy administrator, and the directors of the Bureau of Client Services and Management Services.

Brown looked to the Bureau of Planning, Evaluation and Program Compliance as a valuable organizational unit. Only the budgeting function competed with this unit as Brown's tool for managing change. As one top management staff member noted,

> Brown didn't really care so much about planning
> activities, he wanted to show evidence to the
> department and the legislature that our program
> was back on track. It happened that the planning
> section had the numbers to make that point.

One of Brown's budget specialists told us,

Brown used the budget and program statistics to
learn how the program worked and to argue our
case with DHSS and the legislative committees. Al
[the planning bureau director], Bill [the deputy
director], and I spent a lot of time briefing him
each time he had a meeting with the secretary
[DHSS] or the Finance Committee of the legislature.

Brown stated in an interview,

I guess my style was different from the administrators before me. I wanted facts not folklore to
back up my case. I think times had changed when
I came on board too. Legislators understood evidence. They got impatient with ideas and historical
tales, especially from bureaucrats.

Brown used his planner and his budget specialist to supply
the evidence he needed to legitimate the agency with his outside
constituencies. He used his deputy administrator to help map
strategy. Brown concentrated on control to legitimate the
program to the legislature.

Brown's Use of Innovation

Another major strategy Brown planned and attempted in
order to increase DVR's legitimacy with both state officials was
program innovation. Working with selected central office staff,
he planned a cost-beneficial project aimed at placing a full range
of severely disabled clients into jobs.

Brown termed the project the ERU (Employment Resources
Unit). For visibility the unit was established in Seaside, the
most populous city in the state, with the explicit goal of preparing clients for placement into competitive employment. Brown
also solicited the support of one of the three largest rehabilitation
facilities in the state rehabilitation house to coordinate the unit.

Brown promoted the concept with the DHSS secretary by
stating that the unit's objective was to fit within a statewide
human service delivery system, a concept the DHSS secretary
supported. In a memorandum to the DHSS secretary dated
December 31, 1976, Brown noted that several DHSS divisions
also supported the concept.

By initiating this project, Brown also hoped to develop a prototype program that he could replicate around the state. By accomplishing this, he could facilitate the implementation of the 1973 federal regulations and increase productivity of the agency at reduced costs. The experiment was given priority status and was visibly built into Brown's organizational structure.

Brown's Implementation of Federal Regulations

All VR administrators were obligated to implement the 1973 federal regulations, which lagged several years behind the enactment of the legislation itself.[2] Brown was particularly eager to act on the regulations because he was new to the job. He wanted to prove himself an effective administrator. In addition, the federal regional VR office exerted pressure on him to move the 1973 VR Act into practice. He saw the implementation of this law also as enhancing agency legitimacy at the regional state level, especially since 80 percent of VR funding was federal money. Brown told us,

> I don't think many of the staff really realized that
> they had to change gears to serve clients specified
> in the regs [federal regulations]. Some didn't be-
> lieve they could serve more severely disabled clients
> without more money to do it. I saw it as a challenge
> that had to be done. The regional people were spot
> checking us and our funds were contingent on our
> meeting the requirements.

A budget specialist also informed us,

> He [Brown] wanted to get the field [staff] mobilized
> to meet the federal regulations. I think he wanted
> to have more evidence to prove the agency was
> meeting its mission as well as to show us he could
> do it. But he was motivated in getting along with
> the regional federal staff too. He spent a lot of
> time on the phone with them and meeting regional
> people who came for visits.[3]

Brown did not seem to understand or want to understand, we discovered, the field staff's beliefs and perceptions about the implementation problems involved with the 1973 regulations.[4] Brown's focus was directed more toward external requirements than internal staff concerns.

Brown's Intended Strategies to Implement
the Federal Regulations

We hypothesized that

Administrators who, during critically turbulent
periods, select and implement a dominant internal
control strategy of accountability, increase the
likelihood of motivating their staff to implement
production-related objectives.

Brown emphasized accountability. He also wanted to instill
a sense of confidence in all members of his staff. He told us

When I came to the agency, most of the staff felt
like midgets in a world of Great Danes. They didn't
have the confidence to fight battles with the department [DHSS]. I think they were overwhelmed with
the federal regs and with the LAB [Legislative Audit
Bureau] report on the northern field office. I also
personally believe they suffered from a lack of leadership. They had been hand-held by Adams and believed their program was God-given. When things
got rough they didn't know who to turn to for
direction. One of my goals was to get them to work.

Several of the field office supervisors who served during
that period indicated that Brown tried to motivate them through
more formal production standards, by increasing the monitoring
of their work through the regional administrators, and by visit-
ing their offices to reinforce their responsibility to meet the
1973 federal regulations.

Brown's Attempt to Co-opt Workshop Directors
and County Boards

Brown's uncertain relationship with rehabilitation facilities
in particular and with county boards in general continued to
be a critical issue for several reasons. First, a significant
amount of the agency's direct client service budget continued
to be spent on workshop services and almost half of that amount
was spent in the urban Seaside facilities. Second, Adams left
a historical record as a promoter and supporter of facility
services despite his political disagreements and conflicts with

the metropolitan directors. With escalating costs of services for all clients, Brown was faced with having to renegotiate fiscal and programmatic expectations with an increased and well-organized facility constituency.[5] Finally, the emergence of the county program service boards complicated matters for Brown in particular since he had to define and differentiate his agency's mission and field operations with yet another service provider, and one that was a major user and supporter of workshop services in the state.

We stated that

Major external negotiation tactics based on legitimating and emphasizing productivity will increase the likelihood that administrators will protect their desired organizational domain during critically turbulent periods.

Brown intended to control his relationships with workshops and county boards by developing cooperative agreements with them. His strategy, we argue, was basically defensive—he aimed at achieving compromise not confrontation with facilities over budget and program issues. His intended logic toward facilities was also consistent with his objective of legitimating the agency with external constituencies. Brown adopted this defensive, cooperative position, we maintain, for the following reasons. His strategic interests were to create harmony rather than conflict with outside parties, since his overall goal was to restore accountability between his agency and the legislature. Since one of Brown's dominant aims was also to align his organization more closely with DHSS, and since the DHSS secretary had publicly promoted coordination between service providers and purchasers, Brown wanted to maintain consistency with departmental policy.

Brown, in his former job, had participated in the politics between facilities and legislative committees. He was aware of the continuing influence metropolitan facility directors could exert. It was not in his interest to test or aggravate the already delicate balance of power between his agency and grassroots constituencies. In the end, state legislative committees with ties to facility-supported community advocates would arbitrate the demands of the two parties. At stake would be Brown's credibility as an administrator. Brown, for example, told us

Gates [the powerful facility director] was pretty much in touch with his Seaside legislators during that time. Even though these people [the legisla-

tors] were my colleagues, I didn't want to pit our
friendship against their hometown voters. I tried
to keep a low profile with the directors [of facili-
ties], without giving away our budget to them.

When Brown became administrator, he made Adams second
facility section chief, and Kurt his deputy administrator. Kurt
was selected for this position, according to Brown, because

He was the only one from Adams' staff who seemed
to understand the politics and details of the budget.
Kurt also had extensive experience in the field, he
knew the facility directors and he was liked by most
of the staff.

Kurt was instrumental in helping Brown map tactics concerning facilities and county boards. Based on working documents produced by Kurt, Brown adopted the following tactics:
(1) educate DVR counselors and supervisors to promote DVR's
unique mission, as compared to that of the county boards—
that mission was employability of clients; (2) instruct supervisors
to join county boards and planning committees to target the
DVR client population within their service groups; (3) show
DVR's flexibility and savings to interested parties as compared
with rehabilitation facilities' fixed costs; (4) use the argument
of a statewide organization to redistribute his agency's funds
from Seaside's (the largest city's) facilities; (5) fix and standardize administrative costs in DVR facility contracts to channel
more money into nonfacility client-related services; (6) form
a joint cost allocation committee with facilities to control rising
costs.
Kurt's March 6, 1975 working paper on detailed approaches
to deal with facilities and county boards is informative since it
also shows the strategic logic that influenced Brown's plans to
interact cooperatively with facility directors and county board
directors. We quote Kurt's paper:

It seems critical in my mind that DVR develop some
capability for planning which addresses the problem
of its relationship with the county boards and other
community agencies.
It appears that as the local agencies develop,
and this includes the rehabilitation facilities, there
will be more incursions into DVR money to support
local programming and usually in fixed costs to facilities. The realities of the situation are that the state

will never have enough money to support the programs that are being generated by the county boards.
. . . Obviously the 80-20 (federal/state match) money
provided to DVR will look very good to the State
Department of Administration and other planners.
As I have indicated before, it seems clear that we
need to do a better job of defining the kinds of
services we provide in the community and the role
that we wish to play. This needs to be done in
fairly precise terms so that there will be no mis-
understanding that our role is to serve the severely
disabled and be advocates in the community and
casefinders. This should be clearly spelled out
and we should have training sessions with our
district supervisors and counselors to make sure
that they understand the necessity of their playing
this role properly. Beyond this, we need to interact at some meaningful level with the county boards
in the communities and this would include such
things as having our district supervisors sit on
the planning boards of these community agencies.
It would also require a review of the county boards'
planning mechanisms to see where the soft spots
of the program are in order for us to present a
case for our piece of the action. . . . Additionally,
I think we should cost out our own district office
programs in such a way that if we are ever called
upon to do it, we can show the reasonableness of
the cost of our programs and the value of having
flexible programs such as ours vis-à-vis high,
fixed-cost programs such as the rehabilitation
facilities and other community agencies which have
insatiable desires for money.

These turf protection tactics reflected the environmental
complexity created by the addition of county program service
providers in the state between 1971 and 1975. Kurt and Brown
spent their weekly Monday morning meetings with the regional
administrators, instructing them to carry out these tactics with
the field office supervisors and counselors.

REHABILITATION FACILITY DIRECTORS' POSITIONS

The metropolitan facility directors adopted an offensive
posture toward obtaining DVR funds during this period, even

though the governor had instituted no increases in social service expenditures during these years. Based on our interviews and conversations with 15 directors who served during that period, we summarized their joint positions as follows:

1. Costs for rehabilitating clients when industries will not hire them before training must be shared by the state. Facilities cannot absorb the majority of costs for preparing DVR-referred clients for competitive employment.

2. The policies, rules, and regulations of DVR and other DHSS agencies are contradictory, impractical, and conservative, and do not meet the needs of severely disabled clients in the real world. Facility directors need cost payback guarantees and participation in the policymaking activities that affect their operations.

These positions were similar to those espoused during Adams' term. What had changed were the added complexity of policy regulations from funding agencies and the tactics the directors used to deal with it. For example, the Rehabilitation Facilities Association and the council of facility directors from Seaside exerted pressure on the DHSS secretary to leverage Brown's conservative cost control tactics.

In effect, the two facility associations encouraged the secretary to establish a separate facility services budget line in the DVR budget; to discourage DVR spending in state vocational technical schools and channel more money to facilities; to establish a uniform budgeting year instead of using several federal and state periods, which increased facilities' work with the state; and to reconsider DVR's independent divisional status in DHSS. If the secretary integrated DVR into another division, its funds—so the facility directors reasoned—might have been more easily accessed.

Brown informed us that the facility associations attempted the following pressure tactics to influence the DHSS secretary: they transported clients en masse to the secretary's office to demonstrate the need for more DVR funds; they invited him to public meetings which turned into heated debates over DVR's controlling influence of facility-related policies; and they initiated letter-writing campaigns from their communities to pressure the secretary to pressure DVR to use facilities.

Our interview with the then statewide facility association director confirmed the use of these tactics. He told us

He [the DHSS secretary] knew nothing about facilities or DVR except what he had been told. We knew

Brown and others had his ear most of the time and
that if we were going to influence him we had to
bring our case to him. I'll never forget one trip
we took to his office. We brought a school bus
loaded with handicapped clients and walked into
his office. He didn't know what to do or say. He
had to listen. We applied as much influence as we
could to get the bureaucrats educated to what it
costs to train handicapped people in our workshops.

Some facility directors had a firm grip on the DVR budget
through established DVR field office relationships. DVR client
referrals to facilities also had a history. Our discussions with
facility directors indicated that they did not want to lose the
relationship they had built with DVR.

DEMANDS OF COUNTY PROGRAM BOARDS ON DVR

The emergence of the county program boards proved
problematic for Brown and the DHSS secretary for the following
reasons. First, these boards were grassroots programs that
were partially funded with county taxes. As such, they carried
political clout as representatives of local constituencies. Their
demands for funds often had to be heard. Second, these boards
historically served the very severely disabled mentally and
emotionally ill clients, the majority of whom could not hold
competitive jobs. These boards came to view their mission
and capability of serving the severely disabled clients as more
responsive (since they were located at the local level) than DVR.
Consequently, many boards began to demand more control over
the distribution of federal funds to serve severely disabled
clients at their local levels. Finally, these boards also contracted
services with rehabilitation facilities to train competitively un-
employable clients. Board members began to develop coalitions
with facility directors and argued that DVR was an unnecessary
bureaucratic and duplicative funding source in this service
arena. Locally based service workshop providers and purchasers
(country boards) could, they reasoned, more effectively manage
clients and funding procedures.

Many facility directors also favored removing DVR as an
independent funding source, since DVR's program demands
(i.e., competitive employment) were more difficult to meet
than those of county boards. Also, since county boards were
more generous in paying client fees and were less cost-conscious

than DVR, facilities saw a more compatible ally in the boards.
It should be noted that not all of the state's 72 counties that
had program boards competed with DVR over the control and
distribution of public funds to serve clients at the local level.
Our search through the state historical archives regarding
correspondence between DVR and the boards and our interviews
with ten geographically dispersed board directors, informed
us that between 1975 and 1978 it was mostly the larger boards
that were vocal in their demands to DHSS.

Brown continued to direct members of his central office
staff to promote technical budget and cost allocation compromises
with facility directors. He directed DVR regional administrators
to make written agreements with county board directors, outlining common and differentiated tasks and missions. Brown's
intent, again, was to arrive at cooperative agreements through
joint planning efforts with these boards.

RESULTANT POLICIES AND LOGICS OF ACTION
DURING THE TURBULENT PERIOD

This section examines the alignment between Brown's
observed organizational strategies, external demands, and the
resultant policies.

Brown's Legitimation of the Organization's Image

We posited earlier that

Administrative leaders who can successfully select and
implement production-related objectives and strategies in an
external environment characterized by critical turbulence
increase the likelihood of protecting and promoting their desired
organizational domain.

Based on interviews with agency staff and on our examination of DVR/DHSS correspondence during this period, we found
that productivity was not a major policy objective of Brown's,
although it was certainly a strategy he employed to motivate
and control staff work. Instead, one of Brown's dominant logics
of action was that of legitimating both his administrative and
the agency's image with the governor and the legislature.
Brown succeeded at both tasks, but through conflict and certain
costs to the organization.

Brown legitimated the agency and restored confidence in its operations after the scandal with the legislative audit bureau by successfully using his political contacts, implementing the governor's sponsored reorganization plan through DHSS, demonstrating stricter internal management controls, and by effectively projecting an external leadership image of control. Because of Brown's success at reshaping the agency's image, DVR's state matching funds were continued in the aftermath of the scandal.

Two members who served on the state's powerful Legislative Finance Committee and who had been involved with the report that the audit bureau completed on DVR made the following comments to us concerning Brown's leadership of the agency:

First Legislator: He [Brown] and I knew each other from the legislature. He wasn't a bureaucrat and that's why I believed he got things done over at the department [DHSS]. He always had his facts together and he knew the right people to bridge the two worlds.

Second Legislator: He was a political pragmatist. He always weighed the odds before making a decision. I think he knew he could do the job. He could be tough when he had to, and that's what those social service agencies needed, some-body who could make hard decisions and stick to them.

Brown reorganized the agency in a way consistent with the governor's sponsored DHSS plan. It was, we argue, in his long-term interests to have done so. His strategic logic was to legitimate the agency and restore its operating credibility with the external funders, not to create overt conflict or give the appearance of ineffective administration. The payoff was the strengthening of DVR's image and operating credibility with the Legislative Audit Bureau and the Finance Committee, accomplishments that Brown engineered.

Brown's Leadership Role as Administrator:
LA Career Mobility

We stated that

A leadership style that is technically competent during critically turbulent periods will enable administrators to select and successfully implement production objectives and strategies.

Brown's leadership style was more politically than technically oriented. He used his political skills to successfully legitimate DVR's external image with the legislature in order to protect the agency's state funding base. But after the DHSS secretary left his position and the state for another job, Brown was appointed deputy secretary by the next incoming department head.

Interviews with Brown's closest top-level managers informed us that Brown had intentionally planned his ascent to a higher-level department post while at DVR. We were told by his staff members closest to him:

One Top Level Administrator: Brown wanted a more powerful position to control statewide policy. I think he also got fed up with the planners at DHSS and decided he could run a better show.

Second Administrator: We played with the idea of each of us going to higher positions in the other divisions if he [Brown] became secretary. I think he saw himself building an empire at the department if he got the chance. When he was appointed deputy secretary, he helped get Al [a high-level manager] a position at the Division of Employee Relations.

Third Administrator: As I said before, Brown was a politician first and an administrator second. He knew how to work the system. He was a manipulator who had more ambition and political savvy than anybody I've seen before or since he came on board. He wanted to be governor and took steps to get there. We were one step and the department was another.

While Adams also used political means to achieve his ends, he was, however, more program and prestige oriented in his dominant, strategic logics of action. Adams sought professional recognition by identifying and promoting the program. Brown, on the other hand, was politically motivated to advance his professional career outside of DVR. He used the strategic logic of legitimating the organization's external operating image to build his own credibility. The VR program was, to a large extent, a means to this end. For example, Brown's use of the statewide innovative project (employment resources unit) was aimed, as he stated, "at developing a strong departmental focus on employment." Excerpts from our interviews with the director of the employment unit and other agency staff indicated that this project was poorly conceived ("it was Brown's way of showcasing the agency and that's all"; "never had a chance because of the costs involved and the lack of qualitative client controls and follow-up procedures").

The project promoted Brown's image with DHSS more than it served the agency's mandated mission or clients according to his staff's assessments of the project's original aims and final results.

Brown's Logic of Accountability

According to the agency's major indicators of staff productivity and agency performance, Brown was successful in helping implement the 1973 regulations. The percentage of severely disabled (SD) clients successfully rehabilitated exceeded federal goals (Table 5.2). However, not all field staff reported the same level of success rates.

We asked Brown to comment on the extent to which he believed he was successful in implementing the federal requirements.

> It was hard working with so many of the staff who had their own ideas about work and productivity. Counselors and some of the field supervisors were idealists who wanted to do everything for every client regardless of the cost, time, or effort involved. Many didn't want to be supervised or held accountable for meeting agency goals. But even with these problems, I believe I met the goals set in the federal regs.

Field Staff View

We also posited that

Administrators who, during critically turbulent periods, select and implement a dominant internal control strategy of accountability increase the likelihood of motivating their staff to implement production-related objectives.

We found that field office supervisors and counselors manipulated referrals in order to increase their statistical indicators of productivity.

The ten field supervisors we interviewed who worked under Brown did not believe the actual intent of the 1973 federal

TABLE 5.2

Severely Disabled versus Non-Severely Disabled Clients

| | Year | | |
	1976	1977	1978
National goal for states (SD as percentage of total rehabilitations)	41	45	50
State percentage (SD as percentage of total rehabilitations)	45.2	55.6	62.9
Percentage SD of total cases on record in state	48.3	52.2	51.3

Source: DVR Statistical Records (1979).

regulations could be fully and adequately implemented given the limitations of funds and resources available to them during those years. Therefore, in order to accommodate Brown's emphasis on accountability (i.e., in order to keep their jobs and raises), field supervisors worked to meet the numerical standards and goals set for them.

The extent to which the field staff's manipulation of case-loads negatively affected clients is a difficult research question to address. We shall, however, discuss our assessment based on evidence we collected regarding the organizational conse-quences and costs of Brown's logic of action of accountability after we present our reconstructed policy outcome of Brown's final intended objective.

Brown's Game with Facilities: Compromise

Despite his political skirmishes with rehabilitation facility directors, Adams left a legacy of building, enhancing, and supporting private rehabilitation facilities in this state and throughout the country. Just as important, he left facility directors with expectations that the VR agency should continue the growth-related strategies and personal relationships that Adams had initiated.

Moreover, Adams had actively engaged facility directors in his political strategies early in his term. Consequently, facility directors had been accustomed to dealing with DVR on political as well as program issues.

Brown's plan regarding facilities was different from Adams'. Brown was interested in legitimating the program while enhancing his own career mobility. Toward that end, Brown limited facility directors' involvement in DVR program and contractual issues.

Brown failed in the attempt to coordinate a joint Facility/ DVR committee to agree on the determination and allocation methods of costs to be charged in facilities.

An examination of the minutes from the committee's meetings reflected the DVR staff's desire to define the costs facilities incurred and to determine their sources of revenue. Facility directors continued to distrust the DVR staff motives at these meetings. Consequently, the facility directors did not agree to any of DVR's suggested measures to allocate costs in workshops. The committee terminated its work, and each facility director continued to pressure DVR for funds through their annual contract negotiation meetings.

A second reason Brown failed to solve political problems through technical means with facility directors was his approach. The facility directors had been accustomed to a personal, one-to-one relationship with Adams. Problems had been solved through individual payoffs, side benefits, and informal means.

Brown attempted to standardize and formalize the criteria and methods for distributing DVR's funds and for evaluating client outcomes in facilities. His intentions and efforts ran contrary to Adams' approach. As a facility director told us,

> Brown didn't understand where we were coming
> from. He wanted to do our budgeting for us.
> Facilities are not in business to make money. You
> have to know what we do to understand the costs
> we pay to train clients. That means you have to
> come out, watch our programs, see our clients and
> see what really goes on. You can't do that in com-
> mittees.

A third and obvious reason Brown's organizing efforts failed with facility directors was that the workshops stood to lose more than they would gain. They had already received a substantial amount of DVR's case service funds in their facilities. Helping DVR develop policies to limit their access to clients and funds was not in their interest.

FACILITY GAINS DURING THIS PERIOD

Facilities in general maintained their hold on DVR's client case service funds. Despite Brown's attempts to develop cost control guidelines, DVR's expenditures in workshops averaged over 40 percent of all client service funds spent (well above the national average), as Table 5.3 shows.

It is also interesting to note that in Seaside, the state's largest city (which was also made a separate region by DHSS), the agency used almost 50 percent of its total facility expenditures in three workshops there. These statistics indicate that facility directors in general and those in Seaside, particularly, continued to wield significant influence over DVR's fiscal resources, especially given the lack of growth in this state agency's total budget expenditures during those years (Table 5.4).

Concluding Comments

Based on the evidence presented here, it was evident that the rehabilitation facilities in the state maintained the fiscal and political gains they had achieved during Adams' administration.

TABLE 5.3

Percentage of DVR's Total Case Service Expenditures Used in Rehabilitation Facilities, 1975-78

Year	State's Facility Expenditures	State: Facility Expenditures as Percentage of Total Client Service Expenditures	National Average: Facility Expenditures as Percentage of Total Client Service Expenditures
1975	$5,366,168	39.5	NA
1976	5,584,726	43.4	30.7
1977	5,064,327	43.6	32.4
1978	5,893,351	40.5	33.5

NA, not available.

Sources: Federal Rehabilitation Statistical Guide and DVR agency records.

TABLE 5.4

DVR Total Expenditures, 1975-78

1975	1976-77	1977-78
$25,840,524	$23,924,533	$25,057,989

Source: DVR records.

Brown and the county program boards did not significantly affect each others' policies during this period. While several county boards attempted to access DVR's funds by pressuring the DHSS secretary to intervene on their behalf, their activities were ineffective.

We also observed a closer alignment between facility directors and county program staff during this period. Both parties took the general position that they represented the grassroots consti- tuencies of clients, while DVR stood for removed and unrealistic state bureaucratic control. This was not a surprising finding since our review of 30 facility contracts showed that county boards funded on the average almost 75 percent of facilities' total client costs during this period. County boards, then, looked to DVR to help share costs in facilities they believed would otherwise be added to theirs.

CONSEQUENCES AND COSTS OF BROWN'S
LOGICS OF ACTION

We will argue the following major points in this section:

1. Brown's logic to legitimate DVR with the state legislature by bringing the agency closer to DHSS had a negative conse- quence of alienating field staff from him and his goal. Brown threatened their positions and their sense of historical mission with his logic. Field staff, in turn, lost morale and a sense of identification with Brown's plans.

2. Brown's objective of implementing the 1973 federal legislative requirements by his logic of making staff accountable to formal performance contracts and statistical quotas had the effects of forcing field staff to manipulate client caseloads to satisfy Brown's demands. The hidden cost was the lack of qualitative client services offered by staff.

3. Brown's logic of compromising with facilities by trying to solve political problems with technical means had the effects of turning his facility section chief against him, and of losing his agency substantial funds, which could have, we argue, been more constructively spent on clients in other ways.

4. Brown's logic of using his position to promote his career outside the agency had the effect of leaving DVR more vulnerable to DHSS bureaucratic demands after he left and of disrupting the continuing of agency operations.

Brown's Legitimation Logic: Effects on Field Staff

Brown's actions to legitimate DVR by bringing the agency closer to the DHSS administrative structure proved successful with his intended audience, but sent shock waves through the field staff supervisors. They feared loss of autonomy for the program's mission and for their own positions. Press releases about the scandal in the program and rumors that DVR would lose its divisional status and become a bureau inside one of the larger DHSS human service agencies caused loss of morale, confusion, and anger among the DVR field supervisors. They initiated a letter-writing campaign to the administrator to express their concerns.

When Brown proceeded to implement the DHSS reorganization plan, he demoted all DVR field office supervisors and asked them to reapply for their jobs and to apply for the six newly created regional administrators' positions in DVR. Consequently, several former supervisors became regional administrators while a few lost their former positions. These actions, combined with the staffing of regional administrators in DVR, further alienated field staff from Brown's central office staff and left the agency with an added layer of bureaucracy and administrative costs.

One regional administrator expressed his beliefs that the program ran better with these positions, but the problem was there were so many administrators in the central office who didn't know what they were doing or how to listen to someone who did.

Brown was unfamiliar with the historical context and values that motivated career VR field staff and client-oriented professionals in his state. Whether or not Brown could have carried out his legitimating logic by following the DHSS reorganization plan within the context of a historically conceived core program design is uncertain. The question we asked was, To what extent could Brown have enhanced field staff commitment to his goals by developing a historical core program plan and process that appealed to their professional values? We contend that Brown could have at least achieved his legitimating objectives at less cost to the field staff if he had tried this strategy. In line with this reasoning, we posited the following hypothesis based on the following findings:

Administrative leaders who can successfully select and implement legitimating objectives and strategies in an external environment characterized by critical turbulence should focus their plans around the historical core program.

The other hypothesis we addressed earlier was

Administrators who originate or change their organizational structures by decentralizing and diversifying decision making increase the likelihood of implementing production objectives and strategies during a critically turbulent period.

While the literature describing the conditions for centralizing or decentralizing organizational structures is mixed (Glueck 1980), Hirschhorn (1983:200) noted several important factors that should be considered:

Research on organizational design suggests that an organization's structure must have the appropriate amount of differentiation or division of labor to enable it to cope with the complexity in its environment. Specialization comes in response to complexity. But once an organization has created specialized units or functions, it must design mechanisms to integrate them. It can do this either through conventional bureaucratic methods or through less conventional, but more costly, mechanisms such as cross-functional teams or task forces. Organizations should seek the level of integration necessary to coordinate the specialized activities. Research shows that both too much and too little integration reduce effectiveness—too much would hamper initiative, and too little would inhibit consistency of practice.

Based on our findings, we concluded that

1. Brown had inherited an overly bureaucratized central office structure based on a rigid hierarchical, pyramidal arrangement that permitted limited communication with field staff.

2. Brown, instead of attempting to integrate management with field staff, added an additional layer of administrators that he used to disperse his decisions and to control the field staff's performance expectations.

Consequently, Brown further centralized and differentiated a top-heavy management staffing structure without designing mechanisms to effectively integrate these staff and their functions with the field operations. A consequence was a demoralized field staff with several regional administrators who acted only as functionaries under Brown.

While Brown made these decisions based on his narrow interest of legitimating the agency's external image with its state funders, we asked the question, By what other means and to what extent could Brown have developed an organizational structure that fostered integration between top management and field supervisory staff to meet his objective?

In his new role, Brown was not aware of nor did he use the discretion he had to pursue alternative and integrating internal organizational strategies that were available to him. Toward this end, we hypothesized that

Administrators who originate or change their organizational arrangements to respond to turbulent external events should develop strategies based on the following criteria: (1) Develop a balance between generalist and specialist organizational functions and positions; (2) make staffing changes based on the need and organizational capability to quickly and effectively respond to external contingencies; (3) consider the history and the future of the organizational structure and positions to increase continuity.

The Cost of Accountability

We hypothesized that

Administrators, during critically turbulent periods, should select internal control strategies based on staff backgrounds, expertise, professional experience and values, as well as on the external tasks to be managed.

Brown emphasized an operational, non-client oriented logic of action to motivate counseling professionals whose experiences and values centered on people, skills, and concerns. This logic, to the exclusion of other strategies that match the training and professional values of staff, was not an effective motivator.

Brown's field staff forged statistics to save their jobs and meet federal regulations.

Consequences of Brown's Dominant Use of the Organization

We also hypothesized at the outset that

The dominant organizational processes administrators will use to increase the likelihood of protecting their domain are measurement, control, and production.

While Brown did emphasize measurement and control processes and procedures, he did so not to protect DVR's domain but to legitimate it and his role as an effective adminis- trator. Brown's selection and use of his planning and compliance bureau director (Al), the budget specialist (Ben), and the regional administrators reflected his logic of action of account- ability in choosing and overemphasizing these organizational functions and staff to implement his legitimating objective. By emphasizing these functions and minimizing field operations, Brown's strategies had these effects on the organization:

1. The culture of the organization was disrupted. What had originated as an informal, client-oriented internal environ- ment became a more formal, performance-oriented atmosphere. As Hirschhorn (1983) noted, human service agencies tend to develop cultures that emphasize egalitarian values. Administra- tors who during critically turbulent or retrenchment periods set in force processes and procedures that disrupt these values affect the organization's culture. The costs, as was the case in our study, are human suffering in terms of experienced stress, lowered morale, participation and commitment to adminis- trative goals. Productivity can also be affected. As we dis- cussed, field staff tended to appear outwardly productive, when in actual practice they were manipulating the system.

2. The major direction and mission of the organization was altered. Under Adams the mission was client oriented, even though agency prestige and success were part of Adams' definition of the mission. With Brown, the mission became that of operationally legitimating the agency with the legislature and the federal VR bureaucracy by enacting 1973 legislative requirements. This change of direction at the top of the organization was not shared by the field staff; consequently

the costs were increased conflicts among field staff, regional administrators, and Brown's central office managers.

Given these findings and arguments, the above hypothesis was restated:

The dominant organizational processes administrators choose to respond to turbulent events should take into consideration the effects of their planned strategies on both the internal culture and on the external tasks and mission.

In other words, no one organizational process may be the best to emphasize during critically turbulent periods. Integrating the major organizational units and functional areas to respond in a coordinated way is, we argue, a more effective approach.

Effects of Brown's Logic and Strategic Activities with Rehabilitation Facilities

We stated earlier that

Major external negotiation tactics of legitimating and emphasizing productivity will increase the likelihood of administrators protecting their desired organizational domain during critically turbulent periods.

Based on our findings presented in the last section, we concluded that Brown used a logic of action of compromise with rehabilitation facilities which was to (1) legitimate DVR with the legislature and (2) promote his own career interests within the state government. We noted that he successfully accomplished both aims.

The major cost to the organization of his achievement of these aims was that an excess of agency funds was expended in facilities. Since Brown chose not to check DVR expenditures in facilities, the agency's client case service funds were used at the same levels in workshops as during the growth period. Table 5.5 illustrates this argument.

Regional Administrators' View

Our discussions with the regional administrators also showed that they unanimously believed VR funds were not being well

TABLE 5.5

Facility Services, 1974-75 Fiscal Year

Facility services produced 17 percent of the rehabilitated
closures, while nonfacility services produced 83 percent of
the rehabilitated closures.

It costs $5,965 per rehabilitated facility closure. A nonfacility
rehabilitated closure cost $1,669.

Forty-four percent of facility clients were severely disabled—
34 percent of nonfacility clients were severely disabled.

An average facility case cost $839; an average nonfacility case
cost $179.

Source: State historical archives.

spent in facilities. One administrator in particular reflected
the major themes of the others on this subject:

> I couldn't do anything. If I tried to cut down on
> my district's use of facilities, he [Brown] would
> be on the phone with the director turning me upside
> down. Counselors used them [facilities] because
> they didn't want to change habits. I needed
> authority from central office to negotiate a harder
> line with facilities, and they [central office staff]
> wouldn't come through on that one.

Consequently, Brown's defensive strategies with facilities
proved costly for the agency in terms of funds spent. Given
this finding, we stated the following hypothesis:

Planning major external negotiation tactics during critically
turbulent periods should involve cross-functional teams of organizational staff involved in implementing the tactics. Multiple
criteria should be used in articulating the tactics to include
long- and short-term organizational effects.

Effects of Brown's Leadership Style

Another major hypothesis we presented was that

A leadership style that is technically competent during
critically turbulent periods will enable administrators to select
and successfully implement production objectives and strategies.

No one we interviewed or talked with in DVR disputed Brown's ability as a political and influential leader in the state legislature. In fact, even Brown's adversaries in DVR gave him credit for being decisive and successful in setting and achieving his goals.

We found that Brown's important outside governmental and political contacts and his ability to use these in his position helped him realign DVR with the legislature. This was an important accomplishment since DVR stood to lose its state funding because of the legislative audit bureau's report on the scandal. Legislative confidence in DVR's leadership and management control system was low when Brown came to the job, but when he left he had reestablished the program's operating legitimacy within the state government.

Brown developed a cadre among certain members of his top-level staff who admired and were greatly influenced by his political thinking. This included Kurt (the agency's former facility section chief who was Brown's deputy administrator), Al, and Ben (the budget specialist). Al used these administrators to help him map strategy and direct the agency's field operations.

Our discussion with the regional administrators led us to conclude that they also observed and experienced polarization between the central office and the field staff concerning attitudes and working practices during this period. The regional administrators noted that when Brown first came to the job, he traveled to field offices soliciting and sharing ideas; however, after the regional administrators were hired, he used them not to gain information from the field, but to dictate field strategy.

While Brown managed to legitimate DVR successfully with the legislature by aligning the organization more closely with the DHSS control system, he did so at the cost of polarizing the field from central office staff. Brown's political reasoning and leadership style contradicted the client-oriented background and values of his field staff.[6] The effects of this polarization were, as we showed earlier, conflicts between the central office and the field staff over manipulation of client services.

ALTERNATIVE EXPLANATIONS OF BROWN'S STRATEGIES AND THE RESULTANT POLICY OUTCOMES

Two interpretations of Brown's major strategic responses to external events different from those we presented above are summarized as follows:

1. Brown's logic of action and strategies based on legitimating DVR with the legislature by aligning the agency closer

to DHSS were not choices but outcomes of deals he made with the governor. Moreover, he had no other option but to rely on the DHSS reorganization plan since DVR was a division within that structure. The outcome was predictable: Brown helped the DHSS secretary make DVR more of an instrument of that umbrella organization than it had been. Brown's payoff was a high-level position in DHSS under the next secretary. DVR's loss was decreased discretion to DHSS in implementing policy and control over critical decisions.

2. Brown's choice of attempting technical solutions with facilities was the only available strategy since he was no match for their collective and historical strength and hold on DVR's budget and local client service system. Brown tried to weakly negotiate DVR's interest with facilities via a planning mode. The results were loss of more funds to facilities, dissension of DVR's facility staff over Brown's policy, and the facility directors' continued hold on almost half of DVR's direct service budget. Brown was also a winner in that he managed to promote himself outside the agency with no major confrontations with facility directors.

Arguments against the First Interpretation

The logic in these two interpretations is questionable, based on the following reasons. While we presented evidence to suggest that Brown took the job at the request of the governor, we also showed that he wanted to prove himself an effective administrator to increase his career possibilities. He therefore chose to adopt the DHSS reorganization plan to bring DVR into a coordinated statewide social service system for three reasons. First, the plan was initially sponsored by the governor. Second, Brown initially believed the plan would work. He later had mixed opinions after experiencing several conflicts over the secretary's specific and unrealistic centralization tactics. But Brown was too committed at that point to change direction. Finally, when Brown took the job he was also skeptical of DVR's internal staffing capability to rely only on agency expertise to manage the external turbulent environment. In fact, he distrusted the ability of some of the field supervisors. Also, given Brown's long-term interest of increasing his career mobility, we argue that he sought to satisfice organizational options relative to this logic. DHSS plans were the most visible, available, and promising at the time. Brown used DHSS strategies to meet his own objectives.

The Second Interpretation

Brown's attempt to use technical solutions was not the only available means he had or was aware of to deal with the problems facilities presented. Rather, this was for him the most attractive strategy for two reasons. He chose to initiate cost allocation methods to bolster his visibility and reputation as a problem-solver with departmental administrators. His motives, we discovered, were not only to alleviate DVR's budget problems with facilities, but to lead the way for uniform and joint budget-planning activities among facilities, other DHSS divisions, and county program boards. He expressed this aim to us and it is evident in his memoranda on the subject. Second, it could be argued that Brown did attempt another strategy with facilities. He worked out a joint program arrangement with a large facility to run his innovative project (the ERU). However, the costs and results involved were so prohibitive that he scrapped his objective of replicating the project across the state with other facilities. Nevertheless, he did unsuccessfully attempt an innovative, joint pilot program strategy with a large facility.

Concluding Remarks

The evidence presented in this chapter indicates that our reconstruction of Brown's dominant logics of action and the resultant organizational policies led to the reestablishment of DVR's credibility and unquestioned funding with the state legislature. Brown's administration of the agency also improved relations with the federal VR bureaucracy since DVR statistically exceeded national goals regarding the 1973 legislation. Therefore, it could be argued that Brown successfully aligned organizational resources with external demands to enact effective policies during this period.

Many of the hidden costs involved in the choice and enactment of Brown's strategies led us to more tentative conclusions, however. First, Brown's further alignment of the VR administration with the DHSS machine structure set in motion decision structures that would be difficult to reverse and manage later. DHSS represented a large-scale bureaucracy staffed with planners, managers, evaluators, researchers, and administrators who were poorly coordinated and whose jobs, in many cases, were to intervene, monitor, and control operations of other agencies—like DVR—that they did not understand. As Brown later admitted, "Most of the department staff are hired parasites who only feed off other programs at the taxpayers' expense." The results were less DVR administrative attention given to field activities and more to bureaucratic concerns; more DVR funds paid to DHSS overhead costs that could have been allocated to clients; and loss of DVR administrative discretion in operating the program.

Brown's strategies also negatively affected DVR staff by adding an unnecessary layer of costly bureaucracy (the regional administrators) between the field and himself. This decision created conflicts among the staff and disrupted the flow of program services by field supervisors.

Brown's logic of accountability overly formalized relationships and expectations between himself and field staff and led to a forced manipulation of direct client services by field supervisors. Brown's manipulation of regional administrators also decreased the possibility of his establishing effective relations with field staff and of promoting work based on quality as well as quantity of client services.

This was a difficult period for Brown and DVR. Nevertheless, Brown's political skills and emphasis on technical and control objectives salvaged the agency's credibility with state legislators. Brown's leadership proved appropriate.

NOTES

1. Hall's review of the literature on leadership succession (1972: 260) is relevant here since Adams' legacies led into Brown's term:

> . . . given the important leadership functions, there is real potential for leadership to affect the organization. The exact extent and direction of the effect cannot at present be discerned. One source of the variation in the effect is undoubtedly in the degree to which the organization is already structured and the extent to which this structure is subject to modification. Another important consideration is the extent to which the decisions that are to be made are preprogrammed because of precedent, technological specificity that does not allow for much variation, or the absence of familiarity with the range of options available in a situation. . . . another consideration in understanding the extent to which

leadership can affect an organization is the likelihood
that the leader will be able to convince the rest of
the organization to follow his decisions. It is here
that the various forms of power, including interpersonal abilities, come into play again. Another
factor includes the extent to which the other members expect the leader to influence the organization. If the role is viewed as one with limited
power, it is much less likely to have an impact
than in cases where the leader is expected to play
some form of messianic role.

These factors will be discussed in greater detail in the chapter,
especially regarding Adams' lasting influence on the organization
when Brown took over.

2. The publication of these federal regulations lagged
more than two years after the signing of the 1973 legislation.
This delay was explained in a report (JWK International Corporation, 1978:23) funded in 1978 by HEW:

Why, then, did it take more than two years, from
the signing of the Rehabilitation Act on September 26, 1973, before the official Regulations were
published? There were actually three phases in
the rulemaking process: issuance of interim regs
within 90 days of the signing of the Rehabilitation
Act; . . . issuance of proposed regs; . . . and
the 30-day comment cycle . . . which ensued.
The final regulations were promulgated . . . just
two days before congressional amendments to the
Rehabilitation Act required a new round of rulemaking, ending with the publication of another
set of regulations the following November.

3. This was reflected in our interviews with other members
of Brown's top-level management staff, particularly with the
bureau directors of management services and planning, evaluation of program compliance. The director of the bureau of
client services who supervised the regional administrators
believed Brown was more interested in his career than in the
program.

4. The major thrust of the 1973 federal VR regulations
required the VR counseling staff to show that 50 percent of
their caseloads were severely disabled. What "severely disabled"
meant was not clearly specified. Also complicating the work of

counselors was the requirement that they had to keep detailed case notes on their diagnosis of client's disabilities. Written plans that showed how counselors intended to vocationally re-habilitate clients were also required. With no increased funds to serve clients, accompanied by a mandate to serve the most disabled, many counselors were confused, demoralized, and/or uninterested in being told to do the impossible.

5. The number of actors involved in the VR policy arena with DVR and facilities increased during this period: DVR con-tracted with 15 facilities in the 1960s and by the mid-1970s that number was 37. DVR had one staff member assigned to all facilities in the early 1960s; by the mid-1970s DVR had a facility section with a staff of seven responsible for facility contracting. Also, by the mid-1970s the facilities had organized into two formal groups: one was the Council of Rehabilitation Facilities in the state's largest city; the other was a statewide organization designated the Rehabilitation Facilities Association.

6. Part of the VR staff's reaction to Brown's leadership style was, we argue, what Etzioni (1961) referred to as the strain between administrative authority and professional authority. The former is defined by rational and formal technical control systems to accomplish organizational tasks. The latter type of authority depends on a theoretic specific body of knowledge and common experience as well as a unifying value base to coordinate work. In this situation, Brown depended more on administrative authority to define and direct staff work. His staff, most of whom were educated and trained VR professionals, was accustomed to a professional authority-based control system, which Adams advocated at least ideologically if not in practice. The strain between the effects of these two control systems on staff was evident in the comments of the staff. Even Brown had remarked that "This isn't an agency, it's a religion."

6

Administrative Retrenchment Strategies during the Cutback Period

The third VR administrator, Cane, served during the cutback period, which began in the late 1970s. Cane took office in 1979 not long after his predecessor Brown became deputy director of the Department of Health and Social Services in the state. This chapter describes Cane's interpretation of and responses to predicted and enacted federal and state funding cuts. Of interest here is Cane's observed leadership style and the methods he used to gear up the organization for a historically unprecedented forecasted downturn.

RETRENCHMENT AND CUTBACK DEFINED

We used the concept of retrenchment to refer to Cane's intended and implemented administrative strategies to reduce the size of the VR organization's staff and expenditures. The concept of cutback here refers to the forecasted and actual fiscal decreases in federal and state government allocations to this state's program.

Recent studies have defined and framed retrenchment within a broader process of organizational decline (Whetten 1980; Levine 1978). For example, Whetten (1980) differentiated between organizational decline as a cutback in the size of an organization's work force, profits, budget, clients and as the general climate, or orientation, in an organization. Hirschhorn (1983:2) defined and examined retrenchment and decline in public agencies from three separate perspectives:

retrenchment as a process shaped by emotion as
well as by intellect; retrenchment as a process
shaped by chronic uncertainty; and retrenchment
as a process shaped by postindustrial trends.

Whetton (1980) also noted that there is a discrepancy in
the organizational literature "between descriptions of how
managers actually react to decline-induced crises, and prescriptions for how they should react."[1] This chapter attempts to
bridge the gap by identifying and comparing action with theory.

PRELIMINARY HYPOTHESES

A review of the literature on managerial responses to
organizational retrenchment and decline presents more questions
than guidelines for action research on the subject (Whetten
1980). Levine's pioneering article (1978) is instructive in
identifying generic problems organizations face during cutback
periods. He also suggests practical tactics public administrators
can use to resist and/or smooth decline. Hirschhorn's recent
work (1983) on managing retrenchment in public agencies was
useful in the development of our conceptual statements.
Drawing on these studies, we developed the following
preliminary hypotheses at the beginning of our study to guide
our observations:

H-4   Administrative leaders who can successfully select and
      implement retrenchment objectives and strategies within
      environments characterized as cutback in resources
      increase the likelihood of maintaining organizational
      autonomy and survival.
H-4a A leadership style that is characterized as politically
      competent during cutback periods enables administrators
      to select and implement retrenchment objectives and
      strategies more successfully.
H-4b Adoption of major external negotiation tactics of realigning
      allies and resources, refocusing mission, and emphasizing
      survival enhances the likelihood of successfully implement-
      ing retrenchment objectives and strategies within cutback
      environments.
H-4c Administrators who originate or change their organizational
      structures by contracting size and combining functions
      enhance their likelihood of successfully implementing
      retrenchment objectives and strategies within environ-
      ments characterized by declining resources.

H-4d The dominant organizational processes administrators
will use to increase their opportunities to retrench are
budgeting and political liaison activities.

H-4e Administrators who, during environments characterized
as cutback, select and implement a dominant internal
control strategy based on the historical mission, increase
the likelihood of motivating their staff to implement
retrenchment strategies.

These statements are revised at the end of the chapter to
reflect our findings.

BACKGROUND TRENDS AND EVENTS, 1979-82

The years we observed Cane's strategy formation activities
were the initial to middle phases of a fiscal cutback period that
extended beyond this study.[2]

While Cane's appointment preceded the introduction of
Reaganomics to the social services arena by one and a half
years, in 1979 this state was already experiencing fiscal problems. The rising costs of health care in particular burdened
the DHSS budget. DHSS administrators in turn exerted economic
pressure on the department's other divisions, including DVR,
to share these rising institutional costs.

Moreover, the lame duck Congress that preceded Reagan's
election also caused DVR fiscal problems by holding down
increases in social security program allocations in 1980. In
other words, Cane was introduced to an emerging cutback
climate before Reagan's unprecedented policies were even
announced.

The Federal Cutback Context

The election of Ronald Reagan and his domination of a
new conservative Congress would have a significant impact on
Cane's administration. The greatest threat to the DVR program
came from Reagan's plan to use a block grant for human service
programs. This plan would first collapse various human service
programs into blocks of programs. Second, these blocks would
be reduced at the federal level between 25 percent to 65 percent
over three years. Third, the block programs would be administered exclusively by state governments. For DVR the block
grant approach would eliminate the program's categorical federal

funding status. It also meant the possibility of DVR losing its separate federally based mission. If state governments paid for the programs, they would decide the nature of the programs.

Congress has to date exempted the vocational rehabilitation program from Reagan's block grant proposal. Moreover, Congress has successfully resisted the amount of proposed cuts the Reagan administration issued for the VR program. For example, as of the spring of 1982 Reagan's $767 million appropriation to the VR program was compromised and appropriated at $863 million. The threat of Reagan's cuts have as of this writing outweighed the realized outcomes for the VR program. Nevertheless, the climate of fear and apprehension created by Reagan's new federalism policy were real to governmental administrators and employees.

State cuts to the DVR budget were also problematic for Cane and the agency because these decreases meant the agency would be unable to continue the practice of supplying "overmatchers" of state funds to capture additional unspent federal VR monies at the end of the fiscal year.[3] Agency fiscal planners usually counted on bringing in additional federal funds through this procedure.

Another major economic problem for DVR during this period was the pressure its umbrella agency (DHSS) put on other divisions to help pay for unbridled increases in Medicaid and the overcrowded prison system. As early as September 1980, DHSS assessed DVR $150,000 for the projected 1982-83 biennial budget, to be held as emergency funds for calculated cost overruns in these areas.

The threat of Reagan's block grant proposal jeopardized DVR's historic mission and program requirements, which were largely based on federal legislation. Essentially, had Reagan's proposals passed, the agency could have become a state-funded and legislatively controlled program.

At worst, DVR could have been reduced to an operating unit within a larger division at DHSS. At best, DVR could have continued to exist in a greatly reduced but autonomous program inside DHSS. It was against this forecasted background that Cane made his strategic retrenchment plans.

CANE: FORMER COUNTY BOARD DIRECTOR
AND CLIENT ADVOCATE

We posited that

A leadership style that is characterized as politically competent during cutback periods enables administrators to

select and implement retrenchment objectives and strategies
more successfully.[4]

Cane, however, was not selected by Bill (the DHSS secretary) to retrench the DVR organization. When Cane took the
job, Reagan had not been elected and the federal threat to welfare
programs had not been introduced.

Cane had worked as a successful director of a county
program board in a rural, northern part of the state. It was
believed that the DHSS secretary who hired Cane to head DVR
saw the move as helping to reduce state-local and county board-
DVR differences.[5] Cane had been an outspoken advocate of
clients' rights at the grassroots county level, and he was
program oriented. Cane's background and professional value
orientation, then, seemed a good fit with DVR from Bill's viewpoint.

1979-80: CANE'S RELATIONSHIP-ORIENTED STYLE

During Cane's first year and a half, his leadership style
worked well at the local county level, but it proved problematic
in the more complicated state arena. Upon his arrival, he showed
a sincere enthusiasm (which bordered on naiveté) for the work.
Specifically, he emphasized the central role he planned to give
to clients and consumer groups in his policymaking decisions.
He publicly announced that the organization would be open to
the ideas of local client advocate groups to improve the agency's
services. Cane did not seem to be aware of the diverse politics
of VR counselor-client and field office-central office relationships.
Nor was he that familiar with the effects that Adams' and Brown's
policies and administrative decisions had had on VR staff and
their handling of caseloads. He also seemed initially uninformed
of the tremendous conflicts the 1973 VR legislation placed
counselors in, a group that had to do more with less. He, like
Brown, was initially accepted at face value by the VR staff.

During the first year and a half, Cane demonstrated a
somewhat parochial, relationship-oriented leadership style that
frustrated field and central office VR staff who had been
accustomed to more task-oriented, politically seasoned leaders
like Adams and then Brown. For example, Cane introduced
himself to the job by traveling to each of the 21 field offices.
At these meetings Cane took the role of newcomer and espoused
the importance of consumer groups in the programs. He also
emphasized his role of building on Bill's philosophy of creating
a partnership among local and state service providers and

purchasers. Cane did not realize that to VR field staff DHSS meant more bureaucracy and complications for their program. County programs were not VR supervisors' and counselors' favorite agencies. VR staff members were not interested in partnerships with agencies that had in the past fought over their turf. Cane's attempts at informal and somewhat ceremonial, symbolic meetings created some distance between him and many of the field staff.

1980-82: THE POLITICIZATION OF CANE'S STYLE

Between 1980 and 1982 Cane's leadership style changed; he began to drop his ceremonious style and gave attention to the program and its budget. Because of the declining fiscal condition in the state, the inability of DHSS to control institutional costs, and Reagan's threats to welfare programs, Cane developed a more political style than he had brought to office. While he still maintained his interest in client and consumer affairs, he began to study the distinctive nature of vocational rehabilitation programs. He also began to worry about his job. Some said the political events described above had a sobering effect on Cane.

CANE'S STRATEGIC INTENTIONS AND ATTEMPTS TO MANAGE AN EXTERNAL CUTBACK ENVIRONMENT

Cane's strategic intentions during the years we observed his term are summarized in Table 6.1.

Cane's Controversial Advisory Councils

To include consumers in DVR's formal decision-making process, Cane organized a statewide network of Consumer Advisory Councils. His following statements, made in the winter 1980 edition of the agency's newsletter, illustrate his early objectives and point out his initial problems in adjusting to the complex state social service arena:

It has been almost a year since I accepted the
position of Administrator of Vocational Rehabilitation.
. . . For me, the experience as Administrator has
been a tremendous learning and growing experience,

TABLE 6.1

Cane's Intended Goal-Attainment Activities

Objectives	Related Strategies
1979 (the early years)	
1. Increase consumer and local client advocacy groups' participation in DVR's program decisions.	1. Form and strengthen statewide consumer groups to input ideas to DVR.
1-A Become the lead agency in DHSS for modeling delivery of client services in state.	1-A Cooperate with DHSS agency planning. Implement Bill's philosophical initiatives in the field.
1981-82 (the middle years)	
2. Ensure agency survival and autonomy.	2. Develop and implement an early retrenchment plan before other DHSS and county board agencies responded to cutback forecasts.

Source: Compiled by the author.

one that I expect will continue. . . . I have also
come to know the realities of program budgets,
political decisions, program planning and fiscal
restraint. These realities tend to offer a different
set of challenges; they offer a whole new perspective
to the phrase "service people." Like any other
program, the DVR is a part of a system, a process.
With such a process, there are never any quick
solutions or easy decisions; everything is a part
of a larger network. Perhaps this is the hardest
part of the role I play—striking that essential
balance between people and program.

Cane's success as a county human service program administrator had depended on and developed through his ability to
win support of community groups. Cane told us,

> I have always believed in an open organization. We
> are responsible to consumers and clients. They
> pay our salaries, that's why we are here. How can
> I serve them if I don't know what they need and
> whether or not they think we're doing a good job?
> Besides clients, they are the heart of our program.

Cane's top-level aide and two other administrators involved
in this area believed Cane's use of these boards was a waste of
time and agency resources. One of Cane's staff members told
us,

> I have to go to every damn advisory board meeting.
> We get in the room, pass out the agenda, and sit
> there arguing with each other for two hours each
> session. It's frustrating as hell to me because I
> don't see any results except some airing of rumors.
> I spend almost 20 percent of my time on these
> groups. But he's [Cane's] the boss.

Kurt (second in command) said,

> Cane thinks he's back with the county programs.
> These people [councils] know they can't do a lot.
> Most of them come for a free lunch and to visit.

Serious misunderstandings at the outset developed between
Cane and his staff over the use of the councils for DVR. The
importance Cane assigned to the councils and his insistence on
using them for general feedback caused his staff to question
his sense of priorities.

The Lead Agency Myth

Cane also chose at the outset of his term to strive to make
DVR a lead agency at DHSS. He chose this objective because
he wanted to endear himself to the DHSS secretary who had
selected him. Moreover, Cane wanted to impress upon his
county board counterparts that he could excel at the state
level in another program arena. Cane also respected the
DHSS secretary and initially believed in his goal of creating
a partnership between state, county, and local service providers
and purchasers of services.

Cane's plan to make DVR the lead agency meant different things to different people in his own agency. For some it meant a hell of a lot of paperwork they could do without; creating work plans they didn't need; submitting budgets—pipedreams—two years ahead of time. Another saw the lead agency idea as a way Cane could get strokes from Bill.

End of the Honeymoon

The honeymoon period for Cane ended in August of 1980 when combined federal and state cutback activities led him to rethink his policy directions and relationships with other agencies. In the next section we reconstruct the specific conditions that influenced Cane's later retrenchment planning and his intended game plan to respond to the threat of governmental cutbacks.

Cane's Announced Retrenchment Objective

We stated earlier that

Administrative leaders who can successfully select and implement retrenchment objectives and strategies within environments characterized as cutback in resources increase the likelihood of maintaining organizational autonomy and survival.

Cane's dominant retrenchment objective was program survival and agency autonomy. As early as August 1980, Cane became disillusioned with and somewhat fearful of DHSS demands. Because of rising prison and Medicaid costs in the state, the governor pressured Bill at DHSS to help pay for these costs from agency revenues and funds. These actions caused Cane concern over DVR's role in helping or aligning too closely with other state agencies. "Where and when will our responsibility end?" he asked at a staff meeting.

During the same time span (August to October 1980) Congress passed a continuing resolution that held constant DVR's social security funds. This congressional action resulted in Cane's calculation of a $1 million loss to DVR for his 1980 projected federal fiscal budget. Reagan's election in November 1980 and his proposals for reduced federal aid added to Cane's worries.

Cane announced in an early 1981 section of his agency's newsletter his intention to retrench DVR:

The 1980s—The Challenge Ahead

As is evident in the Human Services Block Grant proposal submitted by President Reagan, an even greater challenge is anticipated for vocational rehabilitation programs in the decade ahead. Our program will undergo major changes within the next few years; changes that may radically alter the way in which VR services are provided. Based on the Reagan proposals and the projected federal appropriations, we cannot rely upon routine budget increases for VR programs; basic survival as an agency may be the biggest challenge we face.

Cane intentionally kept his announced retrenchment objective general.[6] Coalition-building activities in his agency began. He relied primarily on Kurt to help map a comprehensive game plan and set of strategies. He also used Larry, the budget specialist, to provide fiscal data and contingency analyses for retrenchment planning. He used Phil, the personnel analyst, to help plan layoffs. Jack, the VR facility specialist, was used to work primarily with Kurt on planning ways to cut back facility expenditures during this period. The intensity of Cane's leadership activities increased noticeably.

Cane did not, however, use the regional administrators or the field office supervisors directly in planning and developing the game plan. They would implement plans later. The planning process was protected from leaks and, to some extent, critical evaluation.

The Surprise Layoffs

Cane planned an unprecedented layoff in 1981. At least 16 counselors (most in the urban area of Seaside) and only three central office facility staff were targeted. A hiring freeze would go into effect on all unfilled positions. This phase was to be implemented at the end of May 1981.

In February 1981, Kurt and Jack worked on contingency plans to reduce all facility contracts in the state by 12.5 percent at midyear and to terminate at least one facility contract in each of the six regions. Vocational technical school contracts were not exempt from these planned cuts.

The first retrenchment phase was directed at internal
agency layoffs; the second phase was aimed at reducing DVR's
external contracts, primarily with facilities. Both phases were
to be implemented sequentially and without sufficient notice to
the implementers or those affected.

Cane interpreted Reagan's human service block grant
proposal literally, that is, as if it were actually to be implemented
and began planning to significantly retrench his organization
well ahead of DHSS and the county boards. Cane reasoned that
if he moved ahead of the other state and county service providers, he could implement his retrenchment activities as he
chose. He also believed he could show DHSS how retrenchment
planning could be accomplished in a swift, efficient manner.
He reasoned that as the first agency in the state to retrench,
he could preserve DVR's autonomy and unique client- and
employment-oriented mission at DHSS. To wait for the block
grant implementation was to invite chaos at DHSS. He could
only stand to lose ground to other larger, more powerful
divisions in the coming shuffle. Cane told us during the
February retrenchment planning phase:

> If we sit back and wait for Reagan's federal block
> grant program to be enacted, we probably won't
> be around to get reorganized. There are several
> things we can do to protect ourselves and we're
> going to take some risks in doing them. We're
> reviewing our budgets and staffing needs now.
> DVR has a unique mission to get handicapped clients
> employed. We have to keep our independence before
> we can keep our mission alive.

Cane was greatly influenced by statements from Brown,
then deputy secretary at DHSS, on what would happen if
Reagan's block grant proposal passed. Brown told Cane and
members of his staff at a DVR meeting in early 1981,

> If Reagan's block grant proposal goes through, all
> hell will break out over there (DHSS). It's going
> to be a scene of bureaucratic cannibalism like you've
> never imagined. People are going to be scrambling
> for each others' jobs and throats. The survival of
> the fittest will win.

Cane thought, too, that if DVR laid off some of its own
people first, then it could justifiably reduce its commitments to
outside service agencies like workshops.

In addition to Cane's plan to lay off some of his administrative staff, he also decided to demote three of the six regional administrators, thus cutting in half this staff component. Additionally, Cane drew up plans to collapse four of his central office bureaus into two, thereby displacing two of his bureau directors. He made plans to move the bureau for the blind to another DHSS division, a historical decision. The remaining key central office management bureaus at DVR would be field services and a combined management services, compliance, and evaluation bureau.

Cane based his rationale for reducing and consolidating the organization on his belief that the agency had become too bureaucratized and top heavy to serve clients. Cane verbally justified his far-reaching internal organizational retrenchment plans by claiming he was preserving the agency's autonomy within the bureaucratic jungle at DHSS. He also said he was returning DVR to its historical mission of getting clients jobs. Cane's consolidation efforts continued into the first quarter of 1982.

The Second Phase of Retrenchment

We hypothesized that

Adoption of major external negotiation tactics of realigning allies and resources, refocusing mission, and emphasizing survival enhances the likelihood of administrators' successfully implementing retrenchment objectives and strategies within cutback environments.

The second phase of Cane's retrenchment game plan was aimed not at realigning allies but at minimizing DVR's fixed contractual relationship and fiscal dependence on facilities. Cane and Kurt both told the regional administrators and other central office staff on several occasions between January and May 1981 that the agency could not afford to continue purchasing the same amount of services from facilities as in the past.

Kurt took a hard line toward facilities during these retrenchment planning stages. Kurt was a career VR professional. He had done battle as a former DVR facility specialist with the metropolitan directors for years. He seemed particularly eager to make quick and significant cuts in DVR's facility contracts. He stated at a DVR regional administrators meeting in March 1981,

Now is the time to move. In an environment like this we have to cut and cut quick. Besides, they

> [facility directors] are waiting for us to do some-
> thing. It's as if they expect it.

There was consensus among Kurt, Larry, and Cane to take
advantage of the cutback climate to change DVR's funding
relationship with and historical dependence on workshop facilities. They felt they had to act responsibly to protect the
agency in the face of impending federal cuts.

Cane told us in February 1981 that he felt he had been held
hostage by facility contracts. By 1981 he had adopted the position
his key central office staff espoused, that facility expenditures
took funds away from field offices and DVR counselors' use.

In February 1981, Cane assigned Kurt and Jack, the
facility section specialists, the task of presenting a retrenchment plan for reducing DVR's facility contracted expenditures.
We asked Jack to characterize that planning process. He told
us that Kurt decided to terminate at least one facility contract
in each region and to spread and subtract the remaining 25
percent cut needed from the other facility contracts in each
region. He said the facility section staff thought the idea and
justification were absurd. He told us, "I had trouble working
with them on this assignment because they saw no reason to it.
The difficult part of the plan would be to get the field staff to
buy it and claim responsibility for terminating certain contracts
in their region. It was an unprecedented, high-risk historical
move."

Without substantial involvement of field staff in this planning
process, Cane ordered 12 facility contracts terminated in midyear and the remaining contracts to be cut 12.5 percent of their
half-year allocated funds. The total effect was almost a 25
percent cut to facility contracts over a one-year period. This
for the workshop directors was a bomb waiting to explode.

The plan had been constructed between the months of
February and April 1981. The two phases of the plan presented
above were implemented respectively in May and June 1981, only
five months after Reagan's election and before any actual implementation of Reagan's forecasts for human services were made.

1979-81: RESULTANT POLICIES AND LOGICS OF ACTION— CONSUMERISM, REACTION, AND DOMINATION

LA Consumerism: Cane's Use of the Consumer Advisory Boards

We observed that Cane did not involve the consumer boards
in the retrenchment process, except to use them to justify his
plan and actions after they were implemented.

We attended two advisory board meetings shortly after Cane's retrenchment plan was enacted. Cane had key staff members present the rationale and extent of the agency's retrenchment cuts at these sessions.

At both meetings several members inquired why they were not informed or involved in discussing these actions before they were implemented. Cane and his staff expressed at both meetings the fiscal urgency required for their immediate actions. A controversy erupted at one meeting over DVR's insensitivity to the board. Cane relied on Jack, Kurt, and Larry to explain the retrenchment actions from statistical data.

Cane sometimes intentionally and at other times unintentionally manipulated the boards from two perspectives: at the beginning of his term, Cane used the boards as a simple mechanism to share common, routine information and rumors. After his retrenchment plans were enacted, Cane unsuccessfully tried to use the boards as a vehicle to justify his actions to the community.

CANE'S REACTION AND DOMINATION LOGICS

In retrospect, the methods and timing Cane used to enact his retrenchment plans reflected preemptive and crisis-oriented strategies. The strategic principles underlying Cane's actions were based as much on reactionary and dominating responses to forecasted federal trends as on a survival logic regarding actual governmental fiscal cuts. For example, with no intensive prior involvement of field staff in the substantive planning or discussion of retrenchment issues, Cane sent notices to 16 urban VR counselors and three central office facility section staff 60 days before they were to be released on May 30, 1981.

The actual announcement shocked the staff with whom we talked in the agency, including those who had been involved in the planning. No one in the field whom we interviewed suspected such a large number to be laid off. The surprise element of the event also frustrated and angered those involved. Little attempt had been made by Cane to explain his actions, except for the rationalization he used that combined federal and state cuts necessitated layoffs.

Repeated reactions from field office supervisors to us included, "Why had so many counselors and so few central office bureaucrats been laid off? Why had so many counselors from one field staff been cut? Who is going to be next? Why is Cane cutting so many people before any significant federal cuts are made to the program?"

The speculations and rumors staff constructed to explain these actions included the following: "This is Cane's and Kurt's way of protecting themselves and the fat in central office"; and, "Kurt's behind this, trying to get even with everyone he has hated for the past 20 years." Fear and anxiety characterized the agency's internal environment.

Jack, a line supervisor, was notified only two days before the layoff notices were sent to his staff. He told us,

> I was scared to death. I ran into Kurt's office the next day and said, "When are you planning to let me go so I can look for another job?" Kurt looked surprised and told me there was no plan to lay me off. But I kept worrying, why have a supervisor with only a couple of people to supervise? It was a madhouse.

Stress from the layoffs and mistrust of Cane and Kurt were widespread among the field and central office staff.

Several months after this first round of layoffs, Cane announced that only two of the six regional administrators would remain in their positions. Those demoted filed formal grievances against Cane and Kurt with the state personnel commission. Not enough lead time or justifiable cause, they claimed, was given them.

In addition, Cane implemented his plan to collapse four of the central office bureaus into two. Al, who had been one of Brown's favored staff members, was released from his position and assigned temporarily as a regional administrator. Dan, a respected senior administrative staff member, was demoted. Cane's removal of these individuals signaled additional uncertainty and caused stress for many of the remaining central office staff.

Cane followed these drastic actions with another. He brought in a career state employee from DHSS to head the newly created Bureau of Operations and Planning, which oversaw all of DVR's internal management functions after the reorganization. We discussed Cane's action with Rita, an agency planner. She told us,

> They [Cane and Kurt] are unpredictable. We've spent the last few years trying to escape the craziness of DHSS, now they bring them in to run the agency. Does that make sense to you? I'm looking for another job, now, before I get turned out.

Cane's Cutbacks: Too Far Too Fast

At the end of July 1981, Larry, the budget analyst, noted in a memorandum to Cane,

> The Division's actions have generated over 60
> vacancies, as a result of not filling positions.
> The Division salary line is $1.25 million less than
> if the authorized positions had remained filled.
> Beginning with the Federal FY82 the actual salary
> level will be 17% less than full authorization. This
> is a dollar difference of roughly $2 million. The
> area causing the greatest concern for the Division
> is the direct service counseling component of the
> program. Critical needs have demanded that a few
> of·these counseling positions must be filled. Though
> at least 20 counseling positions will remain unfilled
> for this fiscal year. The problem for the agency,
> however, is the increasing caseload that the current
> counselor component must carry. Between June of
> 1976 and June of 1980, the active VR caseload con-
> sistently ranged from 21,000 to 22,000 clients. Since
> June of 1980, the point where we began to respond
> to last year's funding reductions, the active case-
> load has risen to 25,000 (a 15% increase). At the
> same time, the number of counselors and the amount
> of discretionary dollars has been reduced by approxi-
> mately 12% (FFY82 budget $13,603,393; FFY81
> $15,456,467). The average active caseload per
> counselor has moved from 105 to 137, a 30% increase.

It seemed Cane had gone too far too fast in his May layoffs and hiring freeze. Compounding his problems in July were other unanticipated consequences of his field staff layoffs, namely, the remaining counselors had significantly decreased their spending. Cane's layoff actions and retrenchment rhetoric had affected their spending patterns too conservatively. Conse- quently, the agency was accruing a sizable surplus in its pro- gram funds, especially given the other combined program cuts.
Dan, one agency supervisor told us,

> I've never seen a phenomenon like this. If Cane
> doesn't get counselors spending and fast, we're
> going to have to turn back millions to the feds in
> September. Can you see Cane explaining this to
> Bill [at DHSS] and the facilities after the layoffs?

Another problem that had complicated Cane's early retrenchment actions was the fact that Reagan's cutback proposals had
not been implemented as announced. Cane had publicly used
these forecasts as a major plank in his retrenchment plan. In
fact, a 5 percent increase in VR funds had been committed for
1982.

However, for Cane and Kurt the dismantling and reorganization of the agency's overall structure, the reduction of the
facility section, and the staffing component justified the layoff
actions taken. Kurt told us in retrospect,

> Look, we had too many bodies running around up
> here. People were bumping into each other looking
> for work to do. Our administrative costs were
> taking as much as our program funds.

And Cane:

> I believe we have a chance now to give some responsi-
> bility back to field supervisors and counselors.
> Before our reorganization, there were too many
> layers. I think communication to the field will be
> easier and their work more productive.

Fallout from Facility Directors

Less than a month after the DVR facility section staff
made their routine quarterly review visits to facilities, the
facility directors received registered letters from Cane announcing
the cuts and terminations.

We later learned from the facility directors that Cane's
surprise method and impersonal style of handling this situation
was as offensive to them as the cuts. The facility directors'
reaction to Cane's preemptive and impersonal style of reducing
and terminating their contracts was swift.

The reactions from this unprecedented move drew criticisms
from facility executives, state congresspersons, the rehabilitation association, and from the county board association. A
lawsuit was also brought against DVR by the state facility association.

A letter from the state's facility association to Bill at DHSS
was delivered. We quote Frank (the president of that association)
at length to show that organization's reasoning and reaction
toward Cane.

Dear Secretary Bill:

The purpose of this letter is to present to
you the views of the membership of our organization
concerning the action of the Division of Vocational
Rehabilitation in eliminating or cutting facility contracts throughout the state. Fiscal reductions in
contracts are due to begin July 1, 1981 and elimina-
tion of entire facility contracts is scheduled for
August 1, 1981.

We believe, first of all, that the action was
precipitous to the point of being irresponsible.
Cuts of this magnitude which are not accompanied
by careful planning and consideration for the
individuals and communities affected are bound
to have a negative impact on those individuals and
communities.

We also believe that the selection of agencies
to be eliminated and/or cut was largely arbitrary.
We are aware of the rationale advanced by the
management of the Division of Vocational Rehabilitation for these cuts. The explanations offered
to the individual agencies have been inconsistent
and on comparison invite the conclusion that very
little actual rationale was present. . . .

A June 15, 1981 letter was also sent to Cane from the
county commission for handicapped and disabled persons of the
state's largest city; an excerpt of this letter reflects this
group's reaction to Cane's style and action:

It is with deep concern that we, the Milberg County
Commission for Handicapped & Disabled Persons,
protest the cancellation of contracts with agencies
serving the disabled population.

It is a fact that this decision was made as an
arbitrary administrative decision with no input or
consultation from consumers, agencies or other
advisory bodies which might have brought to light
some less drastic solutions that causes us great
concern. We also worry that this could be a prece-
dent setting action.

We realize that cuts must be made and that
criteria was set by the DVR. But criteria without
outside consultation is always suspect. . . .

The number of protest letters from individual facility directors and state congresspersons required two DVR staff members' time during the summer months of 1981 to respond to the protests. County, state, and local human service purchasers and providers expressed their anger and frustration over Cane's timing method of cuts with facilities. At DHSS Bill also became a target of this outrage.

A lawsuit against Cane and DVR was also initiated by a client in one facility whose contract was terminated. The state's facility association joined the lawsuit and supported it for several months. The suit was later dropped, but at considerable expense, time, and energy to all parties involved.

The Department (DHSS) Reaction

Even though Cane had informed Bill at DHSS shortly before the facility cuts and terminations were implemented, the intensity of the protests from so diverse a statewide audience led Bill to send Cane the following memorandum on July 20, 1981:

> Subject: Preparing for the Next Retrenchment Round
> I found the "first round" efforts of DVR to address downside priorities instructive as did you. I want to assure that we proceed to the next analysis and discussion relative to targeting the impact of federal reductions in DVR in an orderly fashion. . . .
> Because DVR does not operate in a vacuum, this paper should not be developed in one. I want you to involve the Division of Policy people and as necessary the Division of Community Service people from the outset. This effort will naturally blend into our broader DH&SS effort relative to federal cutbacks and a fall legislative session.

The memorandum angered Cane. He expressed at a small DVR staffing that he felt Bill was limiting his discretion. He also felt he should have been congratulated on his achievements. Moreover, he was irritated that Bill directed him to work with two divisional staff at DHSS with whom he did not agree.

Between 1978 and 1982, the federal fiscal picture for VR funds had been slowed in growth, but no drastic cuts were realized, especially as had been forecasted by Reagan and members of his administration. There were decreases in spending in state programs after inflation costs were considered.

We found that the greatest actual threats to the operation
of this state's DVR program were not Reagan's block grant
proposals but the loss of federal social security funds and the
state's percentage cuts to DVR's budget.

Cane, between 1980 and 1982, reacted to state and local
social service agencies in his attempts to prepare for federal
cutback and consolidation forecasts that never matured as
predicted. As one of Cane's central office staff members told
us in June 1982, "Cane cut our own throats to keep Reagan
from having to do it for us."

DVR/FACILITY RESULTANT POLICIES

In addition to the social and political outcomes between
DVR and the state's facilities, Cane's actions during 1981 and
into 1982 with workshop contracts drastically changed the
fiscal relationship between these two sectors, as Table 6.2
illustrates.

The cuts made to facilities between 1980 and 1982 amounted
to over $2 million. This was a historically unprecedented move
on Cane's part. Never had such a sizable amount of funds
been removed from the facility sector.

In January 1982, Cane went further. He instructed Kurt
and Jack to change DVR's fixed contracting system with facilities
to a fee-for-services agreement in which DVR would pay for
services actually rendered to clients in facilities. Jack, a
facility specialist at DVR, also set up a competitive bidding
system in which DVR chose selected facilities with which DVR
would send clients after January 1982. This system, Jack
projected, would drop DVR's expenditures to 22.9 percent in
1982 (from 40 percent in 1980).

End of a Game

The game that had been played between DVR and rehabilitation facilities over the past two decades had changed. The
personal, face-to-face negotiations over prior year budgets
had become a formalized, competitive bidding system in which
only selected facilities would be used to serve DVR clients.

The power facility directors had wielded over DVR through
the state legislature had been weakened because of Cane's use
of the economic cutback climate created by the Reagan administration.

TABLE 6.2

Profile of DVR Expenditures in Facilities

Year	State's Facility Expenditures	Facility Expenditures as a Percentage of all Client Services Expenditures	National Rank of State Funds Spent in Facilities	National Average: Percentage Funds Spent in Facilities
1969	$4,117,165	54	2	24
1971	4,009,231	41.5	3	27.5
1972	4,498,723	43.4	2	28
1973	4,543,626	43	4	28.6
1974	4,848,486	55.4	3	30.9
1975	5,018,221	57.6	2	29.4
1976	5,584,726	43.4	1	30.7
1977	4,064,327	43.6	NA	32.4
1978	5,893,351	40.5	NA	33.5
1979	6,590,140	46.3	NA	34.3
1980	5,082,813	40.2	NA	NA
1981	4,156,443	26	NA	NA

NA, not available.
Source: DVR Agency Documents in State Historical Archives.

Cane had devised a clever and somewhat effective retrenchment strategy vis-à-vis facilities that was carefully timed to
translate wider federal and state cutback activities and predictions to meet his needs. He had done so in a swift, preemptive
manner that had costs, as we indicated earlier, but which also
met Cane's desired outcome of changing DVR's funding relation
with facilities.

By laying off members of his own staff first, Cane had
set up a situation in which facility directors could not have
effectively attacked him for making completely arbitrary decisions.
Cane had, in fact, limited the anticipated facility reaction to
one based on his style more than on substance. For example,
the facility directors' use of the allegation of DVR's harm to
clients because of Cane's retrenchment actions did not hold up
in court.

Cane's retrenchment actions toward facilities reflected policies that went beyond fiscally based plans to include political domination of a group of actors that had historically put up a strong fight to be equal shareholders of power with DVR in this state. As Cane told us, he was tired of being held hostage to facility contracts. His retrenchment activities had won him the political advantage over facility directors during this time period.

CONSEQUENCES AND COSTS OF CANE'S RETRENCHMENT STRATEGIES

In June of 1982, we asked Cane and Kurt to evaluate the consequences of their retrenchment activities. Cane told us,

> I have to run an agency, an entire organization. I didn't have any other choice but to make the cuts I did. I know the layoffs were painful but getting resources to clients was more important. I think I did that.
>
> I learned that nobody was going to help us but us. The Department was in competition with us, facilities were consuming our funds, and we couldn't rely on Congress after Reagan was elected.
>
> We did what we had to do. I believe I helped save the program from the bureaucracy that was created before me. I didn't hire the RAs or all the bureau staff. But I had to pay for all those salaries before I made some changes. It was over-time to clean house.

Kurt responded to our question as follows:

> Well I think we showed the department that we had guts. We did in a couple of months what it would have taken them two years to do. Facilities are still reeling from what happened. I don't think they had a clue of what was coming. We had to move quick or else we wouldn't have been able to. We got some deadwood out of our own ranks and we set ourselves up for worse cuts later.

Another high-ranking DVR staff member justified the actions taken based on the federal social security cuts to the program, rising client caseloads for counselors, and rising inflation rates accompanied by no increases in federal funds.

The same staff person had also argued for more central office layoffs before letting counselors go. Nevertheless, she believed the combined actions taken (i.e., the layoffs, position freezes, policy changes, and facility contract cuts) put the agency in a good position to begin 1982.

Other DVR managers disagreed with Cane's retrenchment decisions and the way he handled their implementation. Most believed that Cane acted not in the best interests of the agency but for his own preservation, that he was also influenced too much by Kurt's thinking—which was vengeful—and that he was insensitive to external agency relations.

DVR supervisors in the city of Seaside approved of Cane's handling of facilities since they believed the metropolitan directors had over-controlled several of their counselors' buying habits. However, these supervisors expressed dissatisfaction with Cane's eliminating 16 counselors from their staff instead of spreading the layoffs over the state more evenly. They complained that with the layoffs and rising client caseloads, meeting the 1973 federal legislative mandates would make their work almost impossible.

Field superiors in other parts of the state generally disapproved of Cane's cuts to the facilities because the cuts did not reflect their need and use of facilities. Many disliked the dictatorial and untimely way the cuts and terminations were made. They said they were embarrassed and had unnecessarily been strained in their relations with their own staff and with the facility staff, who were neighbors as well as professional colleagues.

All the field supervisors with whom we talked expressed dissatisfaction with their exclusion from the retrenchment planning and implementation decisions. As one supervisor said,

> They [the central office] expect us to defend their
> decisions when we don't know what the decisions
> are, why they were made, and sometimes when
> they were taken. Why shouldn't we be angry?

Another said,

> I get accused of being a traitor if I question the
> [central office] when I was never informed about
> them in the first place.

Cane's actions were skeptically viewed at DHSS. Bill's top administrative assistant also told us,

> DVR looks at their planning process from a limited perspective. They forget they are part of this Department. We are responsible for their actions. Their latest round of cuts brought a storm of protest that we had a difficult time justifying. We don't want to repeat that experience.

A consequence of Cane's retrenchment activities vis-à-vis DHSS brought increased surveillance from the department and reduced Cane's strategic decision-making discretion.

Facility and community service directors were resentful of Cane's actions. They lost trust in DVR. The directors expressed anger, outrage, and frustration toward Cane and Kurt politically through Bill, county boards, and state legislators. There was a disruption of facilities' handling of clients since their contracts were cut and/or terminated in midyear.

One positive consequence of Cane's activities, however, was that facility directors had to seek more independent means to sustain their operations. Reliance on government funding would be unreliable in a larger cutback environment. As Frank, the director of the Facility Association, told us, "We've learned that we have to emphasize our business over our public sector identity."

Community board directors and staff generally shared facility directors' attitudes toward Cane and Kurt. As evidenced earlier, several of these boards joined the facilities in writing protests to Bill and to Cane.

The boards' opposition to DVR's retrenchment actions can be summarized as follows: community boards generally felt Cane did not share a common philosophy or responsibility in helping them pay for facilities' costs in rehabilitating clients. As one board chairperson told Kurt in a meeting following the cuts,

> Why do you think DVR should be so special? We help facilities because they help clients. We believe you are more interested in helping yourselves.

County boards viewed facilities as partners in the rehabilitation process much as Adams had in the beginning of his term between 1961 and 1965. They could not or did not want to understand why Cane, who had been one of them, did not view DVR's role as an intricate part of the state's social service network.

REVIEW OF THE ORIGINAL HYPOTHESES

We used the following general hypothesis to structure our field work for this period:

Administrative leaders who can successfully select and implement retrenchment objectives and strategies within environments characterized as cutback in resources increase the likelihood of maintaining organizational autonomy and survival.

Based on the results and findings presented earlier, we restated this hypothesis as follows:

Administrative leaders who choose to retrench their organizations should base their search and adoption of strategies on the dynamic interaction of mission, operational, and interpersonal issues. (Hirschhorn 1983)

Cane at times lost sight of the interaction of operational and interpersonal issues in choosing and implementing his retrenchment strategies. Even his consideration of mission issues was overshadowed by some of his fears and apprehensions of what possibly was going to happen to DVR if Reagan's proposals were enacted.

We are not suggesting that Cane's concerns were not legitimate; we are arguing that he did not consider the different perceived effects his reactionary and dominating strategies would have on his organizational staff as well as on external agency relations. In other words, Cane's choice of strategies to respond to the cutback environment did not involve an active attempt to align mission, operational, and interpersonal elements or consequences of his activities.

Some of the negative results of Cane's retrenchment decisions included the alienation of external agencies, the demoralization of most of his staff, and strained relations with DHSS. Cane did not foresee many of the consequences, since he became preoccupied with the timing and implementation of his strategies.

Leadership Style

We also posited earlier that

A leadership style that is characterized as politically competent during cutback periods enables administrators to

select and implement retrenchment objectives and strategies
more successfully. (Levine 1978)

While Cane succeeded in outwitting the facility directors
in the planning and implementation of his retrenchment strategies,
he did so at some costs to the internal organization and to its
external relationships.

We argue that Cane could have been as effective in planning
and implementing his retrenchment strategies had he involved
more competent and loyal field staff in the search, planning,
and implementation phases; and tested external agencies' perceptions of and planning activities vis-à-vis cutback trends
before hurriedly implementing his plan.

Had Cane not isolated himself and his top management staff
in an introverted search for limited alternative responses to
cutback trends, we argue that many of the negative consequences
of his actions could have been averted. Toward that end, we
restated this hypothesis as follows:

A leadership style that is politically competent, and
uses a wide range of interpersonal, team-building, and planning
skills during cutback periods, will enable administrators to
search, select, and implement retrenchment objectives that
integrate mission, operational, and interpersonal issues.

External Organizational Retrenchment Strategies

To structure this part of our research we used the following
hypothesis:

Adoption of major external negotiation tactics of realigning
allies and resources, refocusing mission, and emphasizing
survival enhances the likelihood that administrators will successfully implement retrenchment objectives and strategies within
cutback environments.

Cane's intent was geared to minimize DVR's reliance and
relationship with facilities while the external cutback climate
permitted such an opportunity.

Instead of refocusing DVR's mission before searching for
alternative resources to facility programs, Cane directed a
somewhat reactionary surprise move with workshops that was
interpreted by the state's other human service agencies as a
confrontation with them and clients in general.

Given these observations, we restated this hypothesis as follows:

Aligning internal and external agency resources and relationships should be emphasized before adopting administrative retrenchment strategies. The leadership style as well as the content of retrenching an organization should be considered in planning, announcing, implementing, and following up on cutback activities.

Internal Organizational Retrenchment Strategies

We posited at the outset the following hypothetical statements, which link administrative retrenchment strategies to internal organizational activities:

●Administrators who originate or change their organizational structures by contracting size and combining functions enhance their likelihood of successfully implementing retrenchment objectives and strategies within environments characterized by declining resources.
●The dominant organizational processes administrators will use to increase their opportunities to retrench are budgeting and political liaison activities.
●Administrators who, during environments characterized as cutback, select and implement a dominant internal control strategy based on the historical mission increase the likelihood of motivating their staff to implement retrenchment strategies.

We argued from evidence presented earlier that Cane planned and enacted layoffs and consolidation activities that were aimed at displacing certain positions and individuals whom he felt were not needed in the agency. Cane's actions sent a message to most of the field and central office staff whom we interviewed that created a sense of revenge and animosity. Most of the staff who were released had either experienced conflicts or policy disagreements with Cane and/or Kurt.

Feelings of helplessness, betrayal, and uncertainty pervaded the internal organization throughout 1981 and 1982. Cane made little effort to affect the feelings of instability and uncertainty among staff.

Partial effects of Cane's actions included a stoppage of counselors' spending. Funding surpluses accrued as we indicated earlier, which threatened to create additional problems for Cane. Counselors also began quitting and finding other jobs. This problem added to the surplus of funds and to the increasing workload for those counselors who remained.

Given the observations, we make the following hypothetical statements for future situations:

●Administrative retrenchment strategies affect emotional as well as intellectual aspects of staff behavior (Hirschhorn 1983). Such strategies should, then, attempt to involve and inform all staff affected by the retrenchment process, from the planning to the implementation phases.

●Administrative retrenchment strategies aimed at changing organizational structure and functions should be based on the core program and mission, and a wide range of staff from cross-functional areas should be involved in these changes from the early planning stages.

CONCLUSION

Large-scale retrenchment activities in public organizations that are based on declining fiscal resources are a fairly recent phenomenon (Levine 1978; Whetten 1980; Hirschhorn 1983). There is no one best way for administrators to retrench their agencies.

In this chapter we argued that Cane took strategic advantage of interpreting a forecasted federal cutback environment to dominate both internal and external parties in this state's VR arena and to protect his agency and his job. Cane used cutback trends as a strategic weapon to gain control over forces he feared would consume his agency had he not acted quickly and decisively. Many of his intentions were, however, based on his intention of helping the program. Nevertheless, he cleaned house with many staff who were, according to him, "dead wood" and his perceived adversaries. While he succeeded in achieving his basic objectives, he did so at substantial and, in some instances, unnecessary costs.

ALTERNATIVE EXPLANATIONS

Cane's retrenchment actions could have been interpreted from at least two perspectives that differed from ours: first, it could be argued that Cane did not act from reactionary motives or from interests to dominate, but from legitimate fear and apprehension of the impending cutback events. It was a time of great uncertainty. Cane was an inexperienced administrator. He therefore acted from his best sense of judgment given the expertise and resources available to him.

While there certainly were elements of fear and apprehension in Cane's activities, our evidence indicated that his actions included but also went beyond these motivations. Facility directors, DHSS officials, and other statewide service providers indicated, as we have shown, that Cane's actions overshadowed the cutback events at the state and federal levels.

A second rival explanation of Cane's retrenchment activities was that he had no other choice, given the magnitude of state and federal cuts, but to take the actions he did. Cane offered this explanation at several meetings with staff, facility, and DHSS personnel. Cane's reasoning was that his predecessors had built a top-heavy bureaucracy that was too expensive for him to maintain, given the sudden state fiscal cuts and the removal of federal social security funds. At the same time, expenditures in facilities had reached a point of denying field offices resources they needed. Therefore, Cane was limited to quick, far-reaching actions to preserve the essential field operations of the program.

While there is some credibility to this explanation, we observed that Cane had other strategic options he could have chosen to meet the actual cuts made on DVR. Other available retrenchment options to Cane would have appeared less reactionary and retaliatory to the parties involved.

Cane's Strategic Options

Could Cane have achieved the same or similar results from his retrenchment objectives by having chosen some of the other options that were available to him?

Cane had the following alternative retrenchment options available to him during this period. He could have initially laid off more central office staff and fewer field counselors. This option would have been more consistent with his logic of desiring to decrease the agency's top-heavy bureaucracy. Cane, however, expressed his belief that he needed the central office staff (whom he could have easily dismissed), and those central office staff whom he wished to release had too much seniority and could have sued DVR. Cane, therefore, chose to lay off counselors. Cane could have effected the cuts with facilities in a less arbitrary, more equitable way. For example,

Cane could have informed his field supervisors of the absolute amounts to be subtracted from facility budgets. He could have then instructed them to recommend which facility budgets in their regions would be reduced.

Had Cane used this method, he could have decreased internal staff complaints about lack of their involvement in the planning process; he could have held his office staff more accountable in explaining and defending their actions to external agencies; and, by having involved them in this process, we argue that he could have gained more staff commitment to his retrenchment activities. Instead, Cane carried out the retrenchment planning using a few central office staff, who were largely isolated from field staff input. Field staff resentment, frustration, and turnover were the result.

Cane could have informed DHSS officials, facility directors, and selected community boards of his general intent and need to take cutback actions before he did so. This personal contact, we argue, would have shown his interest in the wider human service community without giving away his specific plans. Instead, Cane chose to partly isolate himself from these parties before, during, and after the enactment of his plan. His withdrawal from these activities implied "guilt by dissociation," as one facility director told us.

Whether the payoff of Cane's retrenchment activities was worth the organizational costs depends on from whose perspective the question is posed. Cane and Kurt justified their actions from the argument that the ends justified the means. Cane succeeded in reorganizing the agency, dispersing some undesired employees, and gaining at least temporary dominance over facility influence.

The costs involved the loss of many competent counselors and central office staff who quit; isolation from many agencies in the human service sector; many field and central office staff who were demoralized by Cane's arbitrary decisions; and increased surveillance from DHSS; or, put another way, Cane's autonomy was decreased in future retrenchment planning.

Cane could have achieved similar results without the harmful consequences had he initiated a wider search for alternative actions, involved more field and central office staff in that search and in the planning and implementation processes, and related to external agencies on a face-to-face basis more frequently both to explain and relieve anxiety, rumor, and threat of his intentions.

Planning and implementing retrenchment activities involves managing the continuous alignment of mission, operational, and interpersonal issues in changing internal and external organizational environments. Neglecting or overemphasizing any one of these dimensions involves problems and costs.

Cane's job was not easy. It is easier to review and judge his actions in retrospect. He showed courage and much sound judgment in his decisions. However, he also acted arbitrarily and in reaction to many external events. He acted so during a period of unprecedented federal cutback forecasts to social programs. For acting decisively and facing the issues, he is to be credited. But like so many public policy administrators, Cane did not effectively evaluate the possible effect of his decisions on his constituencies before he acted. For such short-comings, the cost had to be shared by many.

NOTES

1. Relevant to our study is Whetten's acknowledgment (1980:374) that "there is a considerable need for case studies of organizational responses to decline. Especially critical is information about the choice between alternative responses. It is obvious that different organizations choose different options, but we have little data on the factors influencing this process of choice. Information on this topic can be collected from historical records of organizations that have undergone retrenchment, as well as from longitudinal participant observations. Accounts of how single organizations and entire industries have managed these situations provide a rich data base for the development of inductive models."

2. Hirschhorn (1983) and Levine (1978) have argued that organizational decline, particularly for government agencies, is a trend that will last for the rest of this decade and perhaps longer. Hirschhorn maintains that organizational decline is a result of a larger societal process of postindustrialization. Levine characterized organizational decline (1978:316) as "a symptom, a problem, and a contingency." He stated that decline is "a symptom of resource scarcity at a societal, even global level that is creating the necessity for governments to terminate some programs, lower the activity level of others, and confront tradeoffs between new demands and old programs rather than to expand whenever a new public problem arises." It is there-fore difficult to speculate exactly how long the current cutback environment for governmental programs, including the one in this study, will last.

3. DVR juggled its funds among three overlapping fund-ing periods: (1) state fiscal year, July 1-June 30; (2) federal fiscal year, October 1-September 30; and (3) calendar year,

January 1-December 31, which DVR used for facility contracts. Because of the overlap in these time periods, DVR could use available state matching funds to capture additional federal monies that other states either did not spend or could not provide an adequate state match to receive. This overmatch game was successfully played by DVR for decades. This was the first period the game had been challenged because of decreases in the state match.

4. Levine (1978:318) notes, "Since budgets depend on appropriations and not sales, the diminution or termination of public organizations and programs, or conversely their maintenance and survival, are political matters usually calling for the application of the most sophisticated attack or survival tactics in the arsenal of the skilled bureaucrat-politician."

5. Bill had been recruited from the state university to head the DHSS. He had a reputation for being a competent but philosophically oriented administrator. He was noted for the personal, rambling memos he wrote at home and circulated to the divisional administrators stating his beliefs. He espoused an idealistic viewpoint of creating partnerships among state, county, and local service agencies. His appointment of Cane reflected his beliefs.

6. Quinn (1977) listed four reasons why executives do not announce precise goals: (1) they do not desire to further centralize the organization; (2) they do not wish to provide focal points against which an otherwise fragmented opposition will organize (p. 22); (3) they do not wish to create rigidity by announcing goals that could become difficult to change; and (4) executives wish to defend the security of their plans from leaks to potential competitors. We found that Cane and Kurt followed this reasoning in announcing their retrenchment objectives.

7

Conclusion

The actual roles public sector state administrators play
in implementing and managing policy changes have not been
critically examined. This study has been an attempt to show
how three state vocational rehabilitation administrators managed
external change over a twenty-year period through eras of
growth, critical turbulence, and cutback. We particularly
dealt with the relationship between these administrators and
directors of privately run industrial workshops which train
handicapped clients to reenter the work force.

DIVERSE ADMINISTRATIVE LOGICS

Several important lessons were gained from this inquiry.
The first is that the administrators we observed used a wide
range of logics of action to obtain their policy objectives.
Selznick (1957) had noted that organizational leaders pursue
strategic means other than those related to efficiency and technical concerns. More recently, Karpik (1978), in his study of
multinational corporations also made this observation by presenting several types of logics of action, which, for example, included
power and prestige. We argued in this study that Adams, the
first administrator, used such strategic means as accommodation,
competition, and coercion to reach his objective to expand the
program during a growth era. He began his term by building
coalitions with groups who assisted him with his expansionist
aims. He later competed with the same groups over the distribution of resources and policy turf. Adams was a charismatic

program zealot whose empire-building activities paid off in many ways. The side effects of his policies, however, led to serious control problems in the organization.

Brown, the second administrator, used the logics of legitimation, career mobility, accountability, and compromise to manage the turbulent environment in the state. He accepted the position to quell a crisis that had resulted from Adams' administration and to enhance his career mobility within the social service sector. He almost gave the store away to groups that threatened his intended goals of legitimating the program with state legislators. His management of the turbulent external events was, however, effective. He helped bring the agency through a transition from a traditional to a politically managed organization.

Cane, the third administrator, used administrative logics based on consumerism, reaction, and domination to implement his retrenchment objectives. Later in his term, when Reaganomics threatened his program budget, he responded to fiscal cutback forecasts with a logic based on domination to ensure his program's funding survival and to curtail long-standing dependence on outside vendors. Cane overwhelmed his constituents and his staff with the speed and magnitude of his retrenchment actions. The fallout and reaction to his management of cutback were, however, damaging to the external image of the program. These three administrators, then, used a wide range of social, political, and economic logics and strategies in their policy formation activities.

ADMINISTRATIVE DISCRETION

A second lesson gained from the study is that public sector state administrators have and use considerable discretion in interpreting and implementing federal legislation. Stewart (1975) and McLanahan (1979) argued this point against the transmission belt model of public administration, which assumed that public officials implemented congressional laws as if these were written on the books. We found that most federal VR legislation was vague and unenforceable. Also, because of the uncertainty and confusion created over changing external events and shifting state and local coalitions that competed over federal funds, the administrators we observed were able to interpret events with much discretion and to impose their policy interests on their staff. Adams, for example, interpreted federal legislation largely in terms of expansion for his program. Brown mapped a course of events that favored his own career mobility within the state social service system. Cane used strategies to neutralize federal legislative threats before these materialized and affected his program interests.

Each of the administrators, then, understood and acted on the discretion available in his particular situation to manage change, uncertainty, and opportunity as they perceived them from their backgrounds, leadership styles, and interests. Adams, for example, interpreted his position as statesman to initiate coalitions in order to assemble a large, field-oriented program and staff. Brown used his former reputation and contacts as a powerful state legislator to gain legitimacy from government officials. Cane used the authority vested in his position to implement swift and unprecedented retrenchment objectives to save his program niche in the state, as well as his position.

UNPLANNED CONSEQUENCES

Another significant finding was that these public administrators implemented strategies and objectives that had consequences that extended beyond their intentions and control. We observed that Adams, Brown, and Cane were more action than planning oriented in their strategy-making activities. They often acted opportunistically to implement their policy choices, without taking time to consider consequences of their moves for several reasons.

First, they did not believe in nor were they trained in systematic planning procedures. Adams was a former field counselor and supervisor. Brown was a politician. Cane had been a county program director and client advocate. All acted according to their own experiences and intuition. Second, these administrators did not trust the state governing system or actors in the system in which they worked. They believed the system was politically oriented; therefore, each acted to protect and further his own professional and program interests. Defining allies and adversaries and deciding whom to include or exclude from their strategic moves often took priority over technical planning activities. We are not suggesting that the administrators did not lay out different options and use contingency data to make decisions. They did. Our point is that they did not follow formal planning models to systematically examine the possible consequences of their actions and revise their plans with that information.

THE ORGANIZATION AS A SOCIO-POLITICAL ARENA

A fourth lesson from the study was that we found the image of the focal organization to be more like a socio-political arena than a machine bureaucracy. State public sector agencies are competitive arenas of actors (Crozier and Friedberg 1977) in which policy directives are essentially adopted and negotiated by top administrators with limited input from selected staff. The external organizational boundaries were also largely defined by the negotiated interactions and outcomes between the administrators and particular external groups who exerted enough power to make themselves heard. Adams, for example, initially included facility directors in his inner administrative circle. Brown and Cane, on the other hand, tried to move these directors and their constituencies away from critical decision-making activities. Adams separated the agency from the vocational education board and joined the DHSS network of social services. In other words, the social, political, and economic boundaries of the organization shifted with the administrators' interpretations of external events and with their strategies and stakes in the policy game played with other powerful groups.

POWER OF ADMINISTRATIVE LOGICS OF ACTION

The organization was observed as a socio-political arena of actors and organizational structure, tasks, and program priorities were seen as driven by the top administrators' strategic decisions and choices of coalitions to manage changing external trends. Adams, for example, promoted the facility section chief and isolated his top-level planner, who disagreed with his expansionist decisions. He also emphasized field office activities. Brown, on the other hand, elevated central office planners and generally deemphasized the importance of field staff in his decision-making activities. He sought legitimation from state politicians, not expansion in the field. He therefore selected staff and a structure to help him and the program appear publicly accountable. Cane reduced his staff in the field and consolidated his central office structure according to his retrenchment aims. Budgeting and personnel functions became key activities in his organizational logic. Many of these logics and actions were based on arbitrary political as well as programmatic motives.

THE HUMAN ELEMENT IN LEADERSHIP

From this perspective of organizations, we also learned that administrators are human beings as well as officeholders. They have biases, overlook detail, and often have a reliance on staff based on trust and loyalty as well as expertise. The administrators used experience more than planning processes to make decisions. Their strategy-making activities sometimes involved them in scandal, conflict, and lawsuits as well as career promotions, increased prestige, and higher salaries.

Their leadership styles varied with their backgrounds and responses to external contingencies. We found that a charismatic leadership style as defined by Katz and Kahn (1978) assisted Adams in finding and developing resources to expand his program during a growth period. However, the down side of Adams' charisma was his unwillingness and inability to share power and authority with competent staff who could have assisted him in making the program accountable.

Brown's political leadership style effectively helped him link the agency to influential state congresspersons and thereby regain much of the program's credibility, which was harmed after Adams' term. However, Brown compromised many of the program's long-term goals in favor of short-term career mobility interests.

Cane's style was also characterized as political. Cane relied on a dominant coalition inside the organization to assist in cutting back staff and decreasing the agency's dependence on external alliances. Cane's retrenchment actions appeared effective in the short-term. A question we raised was how effective would Cane's political leadership style be in the long term, especially given the radical and alienating strategic moves he made with statewide groups during the early years of his administration.

METHODOLOGY: LIMITATIONS AND LESSONS

Examining real-time actions of individual administrators and comparing their management intentions to observed outcomes is a tedious task. Methodologically, there are many shortcomings to such an endeavor. We did not, for example, provide a comparative context in which to determine whether or not the leadership strategies identified in this study were unique to this sample and situation. Nor were we able to identify or substantiate generic conditions under which particular leadership styles and strategies were more or less effective or suitable. Strategies that worked for Adams, Brown, and Cane, for example, may have failed for other VR administrators in other parts of the country during this same time period.

Another limitation was the type of hypotheses used. Our statements were definitional and ideographic. We could at best describe, not predict, alignments between the administrators' strategies, leadership styles, and external conditions. Because these hypotheses were neither causally derived nor falsifiable as stated, our conclusions had to be evaluated as insights and not predictions.

The use of our qualitative methodology also required an excessive amount of time, energy, and some risk. More than two years was spent attending meetings, traveling, talking to and interviewing staff, and taking voluminous notes. Judgments had to be made regarding the protection of individuals and groups who were involved in controversies. We continually cross-referenced our interview results to determine the validity of statements and perceptions as best as possible. At the same time, part of our aim was to present the different perceptions and intentional aims of particular individuals and groups. In this type of research, relating the different actors' stands and views was an important part of the design.

The qualitative methodology we used did provide useful insights into the process through which organizational leaders adopt and enact their strategic aims. By extending Karpik's logics of action concept (which he applied to multinational corporations) we were able to present several diverse concepts from the strategic management literature into a single analytic framework. For example, we were able to separate and describe the different administrators' intended and implemented objectives (ends) and strategies (means). Also, the use of this framework enabled us to examine multiple strategies of each administrator over time.

In addition, by using Allison's concept of game within this goal-attainment framework, we could identify and trace the source, transformation, and results of the policy negotiations between the administrators and external groups. In particular, the changing policy games between the VR administrators and the rehabilitation facility directors were described.

ORIGINAL RESEARCH QUESTIONS READDRESSED

The central research question we addressed at the outset of this study was, Do top-level organizational leaders make a difference in shaping and implementing major policies? We also asked, to what extent do environmental influences affect an organization's policy outcomes? Our findings indicated that the three administrators' leadership styles and strategic activities significantly affected both internal organizational processes and resultant policies.

All three administrators were observed to have developed and used dominant logics to interpret external events and to control organizational activities to implement their policy and professional interests. These social, political, and economic logics changed with the administrators' coalitional alignments, their particular career aims, and with their interpretations of changing external trends. We did find that their strategic logics guided their use of organizational resources to manage change as well as to implement their interests.

Resultant policies during all three administrators' terms were traced and linked to their predominant strategic logics, their leadership styles, and their particular interpretations of external trends and events. Not all of their intended actions resulted in the consequences they would have preferred, yet we found that their major strategic activities profoundly affected their organization's policy outcomes. Adams obtained significant expansion at the expense of some scandal in the program. Brown regained legitimacy for the program with the state legislature and he obtained a high position in the social service bureaucracy. Cane significantly trimmed his bureaucracy and decreased his dependency on outside contracted vendor relationships while alienating many of them.

In agreement with Katz and Kahn (1978:532) we also observed that the three administrators exerted significant influence over the actual behavior of organizational participants. As Katz and Kahn noted, leaders play an important role through their interpretation, adaptation, and embellishment or thoughtful omission of critical work. Power is not equally distributed in organizations. Leadership style and skills are needed to guide and structure decisions. Adams used charisma. Brown used political skills. Cane used coalitional skills and the position power vested in his federal mandate. Each administrator used his particular leadership style and skills to control information and shape staff behavior to implement specific objectives.

The effects of leadership influences on resultant policies were also observed in the boundary-spanning activities each administrator performed. Katz and Kahn noted, "Leadership emerges as individuals take charge of relating a unit or sub-system to the external structure or environment. Where no formal role has been designated for a leader, an informal one

arises especially for those at juncture points in the system
(1978:532).

In answer to the question, To what extent do environmental
influences affect an organization's policy outcomes? we made the
following observations. First, while external events played an
important role in the administrators' strategy formation processes,
it was the mediation of these events through the leaders' particular logics that determined how events were acted on. Second,
we found that external events were part of a political process
in which constraints and opportunities were functions of the
power exercised by the decision makers (Child 1972:16). Events
as such became interpreted elements in the game played by the
major actors in negotiations over resources and influences. For
example, President Reagan's forecasted cuts to social programs
became part of Cane's plan to retrench his agency and to deal
with outside vendors. While external events seem to have a
life of their own, it is the acted-on interpretation of events by
powerful leaders that determines the nature and effect on them
for the organization.

These findings further suggest that proponents of the
resource dependency perspective (Pfeffer and Salancik), the
natural selection view (Aldrich), and the "garbage can" model
of organizations (Cohen, March, and Olsen) have unrealistically
portrayed and overemphasized the powerless symbolic role of
leadership in affecting organizational policy, the lack of individual
leadership volition and intention in selecting and implementing
strategic options, and the overconstraining influences of external
events on strategy formation processes.

Results from this study indicate a different view of organizations and power that organizational individuals and groups
have and use. Organizational leaders have their own agendas
and interpretations of events, which they use to impose their
interests over the organization and over other actors in the
policy arena. Moreover, the image of organizations is most
realistically depicted as interactive human systems with external
constituencies, each competing for scarce resources and influence.
Such a perspective calls for action research methods that enable the observer to describe and understand the intentions,
actions, and results of the negotiations of the various participants in the policymaking process.

In conclusion, we offer the following generalizations resulting from our findings:

1. Organizations do not have strategies; individuals and
coalitions do.

2. Individual organizational leaders' strategies are a function of their professional backgrounds, values, ideologies, and interests (Gallie 1978).

3. Organizational leaders' strategies are also conditioned by political, historical, social, and economic factors that originate internally and externally to their organizations (Karpik 1978).

4. Organizational leaders affect the implementation of policies in the following ways: (a) through their selection and choice of external trends and events to be influenced (Child 1972); (b) through their choice of organizational actors, coalitions, and functions with which to implement policy choices; (c) through their decision rules and control of information inside their organizations (March and Simon 1958); (d) through the tactics they use with external players to implement strategies (Levine 1978).

5. Administrative strategies have costs and unintended consequences that affect actors in the policy arena in different ways. Administrators can enhance their understanding of such costs and minimize negative consequences to widen organizational interests by (a) planning and implementing an integrated search for alternative strategies; (b) involving allies and rivals inside and outside the organization in such a search; (c) developing strategies that integrate organizational mission issues with operational and interpersonal concerns.

These generalizations are not really new. Our message, however, is that they have not been widely or systematically applied to study policymaking activities in the upper echelons of organizations.

Bibliography

Aldrich, Howard. 1972. "An Organization-Environment Perspective on Cooperation and Conflict in the Manpower Training System." In Conflict and Power in Complex Organizations, edited by A. Negandhi (Kent, OH: Center for Business and Economic Research), pp. 11-37.

____. 1979. Organizations and Environments (Englewood Cliffs, NJ: Prentice-Hall).

Aldrich, Howard and J. Pfeffer. 1976. "Environments of Organizations." Annual Review of Sociology 2:79-105.

Allison, Graham. 1971. Essence of Decision: Explaining the Cuban Missile Crisis (Boston, MA: Little, Brown).

Andrews, Kenneth. 1971. The Concept of Corporate Strategy (Homewood, IL: Dow-Jones-Irwin).

Argyris, Chris. 1962. Interpersonal Competence and Organizational Effectiveness (Homewood, IL: Dorsey Press).

Bain, J. S. 1959. Industrial Organization (New York: Wiley).

Baldridge, J. 1971. Power and Conflict in the University (New York: John Wiley).

Bardach, Eugene. 1977. The Implementation Game: What Happens after a Bill Becomes a Law (Cambridge, MA: MIT Studies in American Politics and Public Policy).

Benson, J. Kenneth. 1975. "The Interorganizational Network as a Political Economy." Administrative Science Quarterly 20: 229-49.

____. 1977. "Innovation and Crisis in Organizational Analysis." Sociological Quarterly 18, no. 1:3-16.

Berscheid, Ellen and E. Walster. 1969. Interpersonal Attraction (Reading, MA: Addison-Wesley).

193

Blau, P. and R. Scott. 1962. Formal Organizations (San Francisco, CA: Chandler).

Boudon, Raymond. 1982. The Unintended Consequences of Social Action (New York: St. Martha's Press).

Bower, Joseph and Y. Doz. 1979. "Strategy Formulation: A Social and Political Process." In Strategic Management, edited by D. Schendel and C. Hofer (Boston, MA: Little, Brown), pp. 152-66.

Bucher, R. 1970. "Social Process and Power in a Medical School." In Power in Organizations, edited by Mayer N. Zald (Nashville, TN: Vanderbilt University Press), pp. 3-48.

Burns, T. and G. Stalker. 1961. The Management of Innovation (London: Tavistock).

Burns, T. 1966. Preface to second edition of Burns and Stalker, The Management of Innovation.

Canon, Thomas. 1968. Business Strategy and Policy (New York: Harcourt Brace Jovanovich).

Chandler, Alfred. 1969. Strategy and Structure (Cambridge, MA: MIT Press).

Child, John. 1972. "Organizational Structure, Environment and Performance: The Role of Strategic Choice." Sociology 6, no. 1:1-22.

Cohen, Michael and J. Olsen. 1972. "A Garbage Can Model of Organizational Choice." Administrative Science Quarterly 17:1-25.

____. 1974. Leadership and Ambiguity: The American College President (New York: McGraw-Hill).

Crozier, Michael and E. Friedberg. 1977. L'Acteur et le Système: les Contraintes de l'Action Collective (Paris: Editions de Seuil).

Cyert, Richard and J. March. 1963. A Behavioral Theory of the Firm (Englewood Cliffs, NJ: Prentice Hall).

Dill, William. 1958. "Environment as an Influence on Managerial Autonomy." Administrative Science Quarterly 1:409-43.

Downs, Anthony. 1967. Inside Bureaucracy (Boston, MA: Little, Brown).

Edwards, Richard. 1977. Contested Terrain: The Transformation of the Workplace in America (New York: Basic Books).

Etzioni, Amitai. 1961. A Comparative Analysis of Complex Organizations (New York: The Free Press).

Festinger, Leon. 1954. "A Theory of Social Comparison Process." Human Relations 7:117-40.

Fiedler, F. E. 1966. "The Contingency Model: A Theory of Leadership Effectiveness." In Basic Studies in Social Psychology, edited by H. Proshansky and B. Seidenberg (New York: Holt, Rinehart and Winston), pp. 538-51.

Flanagan, J. C. 1958. "Defining the Requirements of the Executive's Job." Personnel 28:28-35.

Freedman, Sara and R. Keller. 1981. "The Handicapped in the Work Force." Academy of Management Review 6, no. 3: 449-58.

Fruhan, William. 1972. The Fight for Competitive Advantage: A Study of U.S. Domestic Truck Airlines (Cambridge, MA: Harvard University Press).

Gallie, Duncan. 1978. In Search of the New Working Class (London: Cambridge University Press).

Gellman, W. 1973. "Fundamentals of Rehabilitation." In Rehabilitation Practices with the Disabled, edited by J. F. Garrett and E. Levine (New York: Columbia University Press).

Glueck, William. 1980. Business Policy and Strategic Management. New York: McGraw Hill.

Goldman, Paul and D. Van Houten. 1977. "Managerial Strategies and the Worker: A Marxist Analysis of Bureaucracy." The Sociological Quarterly 18:108-15.

Greenleigh Associates, Inc. 1975. The Role of the Sheltered
Workshops in the Rehabilitation of the Severely Handicapped
(New York).

Gutman, P. 1964. "Strategies for Growth." California Management Review 6:31-36.

Hage, Jerald and R. Dewar. 1973. "Elite Values, Social Structure, and Organizational Performance." Administrative Science
Quarterly 18:279-90.

Hall, Richard. 1972. Organizations, Structure, and Process
(Englewood Cliffs, NJ: Prentice-Hall).

Hall, Richard and Robert Quinn. 1983. Organizational Theory
and Public Policy (Beverly Hills, CA: Sage).

Hambrick, Donald. 1981. "Environment, Strategy, and Power
Within Top Management Teams." Administrative Science
Quarterly 26:253-76.

Hambrick, Donald and C. Snow. 1980. "Measuring Organizational
Strategies: Some Theoretical and Methodological Problems."
Academy of Management Review 5:527-38.

Hatten, K. and D. Schendel. 1977. "Heterogeneity Within an
Industry: Firm Conduct in the U.S. Brewing Industry,
1952-71." Journal of Industrial Economics 26:97-113.

Hirsch, Paul. 1969. The Structure of the Popular Music Industry
(Ann Arbor, MI: University of Michigan Survey Research
Center).

Hirschhorn, Larry and Associates. 1983. Cutting Back,
Retrenchment and Redevelopment in Human and Community
Services (San Francisco, CA: Jossey-Bass).

Hofer, C. W. 1977. "Conceptual Constructs for Formulating
Corporate Business Strategies." ICCH no. 9-378-754, p. 33.

Jauch, Lawrence and R. Osborn. 1981. "Toward an Integrated
Theory of Strategy." Academy of Management Review 6, no.
3:491-591.

JWK International Corporation. 1978. "Analysis of Policy
Development and Promulgation Problems in the State/Federal

Vocational Rehabilitation System." Contract no. HEW-105-77-4014 (Annandale, VA).

Karpik, Lucien. 1972a. "Sociologie, economie, politique et buts des organisations de production." Revue Français de Sociologie 13:299-324.

____. 1972b. "Les politiques et les logiques d'action de la grande entreprise industrielle." Sociologie du Travail 1: 82-105.

____. 1972c. "Multinational Enterprises and Large Technological Corporations." Translated from Revue Economique 23:1-46.

____. 1972d. "Technological Capitalism." Translated from Sociologie du Travail 13:2-34.

____. 1978. In Organization and Environment: Theory, Issues and Reality, edited by Lucien Karpik (Beverly Hills, CA: Sage).

Katz, D. and R. Kahn. 1978. The Social Psychology of Organizations, 2d ed. (New York: John Wiley).

Kay, B. R. 1959. "Key Factors in Effective Foreman Behavior." Personnel 36:25-31.

Khandwalla, Pradip. 1976. "Some Top Management Styles, Their Context and Performance." Organization & Administrative Sciences 7, no. 4:21-39.

Kimberly, John. 1975. "Environmental Constraints and Organizational Structure: A Comparative Analysis of Rehabilitation Organization." Administrative Science Quarterly 20:1-9.

____. 1976. "Issues in the Design of Longitudinal Organizational Research." Sociological Methods & Research 4, no. 3:321-47.

Kimberly, J., R. Miles, and Associates. 1980. The Organizational Life Cycle (San Francisco, CA: Jossey-Bass).

Lawrence, P. and J. Lorsch. 1967. Organizations and Environment (Boston, MA: Harvard Graduate School of Business Administration).

Levine, C. H. 1978. "Organizational Decline and Cutback Management." Public Administration Review 38:316-25.

Lieberson, Stanley and J. O'Connor. 1972. "Leadership and Organizational Performance: A Study of Large Corporations." American Sociological Review 37:117-30.

Likert, Rensis. 1961. The Human Organization (New York: McGraw-Hill).

Lindblom, Charles. 1959. "The Science of Muddling Through." Public Administration Review 19:79-88.

MacMillan, Ian. 1978. Strategy Formulation: Political Concepts (St. Paul, MN: West).

March, James. 1978. "Bounded Rationality, Ambiguity, and the Engineering of Choice." Bell Journal of Economics 9:587-608.

March, James and H. Simon. 1958. Organizations (New York: John Wiley).

McLanahan, Sara. 1979. "Participation, Discretion, and Accountability: Issues in Program Implementation." Ph.D. dissertation, University of Texas at Austin.

McGregor, Douglas. 1960. The Human Side of Enterprise (New York: McGraw-Hill).

McNeil, Kenneth. 1978. "Understanding Organizational Power: Building on the Weberian Legacy." Administrative Science Quarterly 23:65-89.

Merton, Robert. 1957. Social Theory and Social Structure (Glencoe, IL: The Free Press).

Meyer, Marshall. 1978. "Leadership and Organizational Structure." In Environments and Organizations, edited by Marshall Meyer & Associates (San Francisco: Jossey-Bass).

Miles, Raymond and C. Snow. 1978. Organizational Strategy, Structure, and Process (New York: McGraw-Hill).

Miles, Robert. 1982. Coffin Nails and Corporate Strategies (Englewood Cliffs, NJ: Prentice-Hall).

"Minimal Wage: Some Workshops Pay Handicapped As Little As 10 Cents An Hour." Wall Street Journal, October 19, 1979, pp. 1, 16.

Mintzberg, Henry. 1972. "Research on Strategy Making." Proceedings of the Academy of Management.

_____. 1973. The Nature of Managerial Work (New York: Harper & Row).

_____. 1978. "Patterns In Strategy Formation." Management Science 24:934-48.

_____. 1983. Power In and Around Organizations (Englewood Cliffs, NJ: Prentice-Hall).

Nelson, N. 1971. Workshops for the Handicapped in the United States: An Historical and Developmental Perspective (Springfield, IL: Charles C. Thomas).

Normann, R. 1969. "Organization Mediation and Environment." SIAR report no. UPM-RN-91 (Stockholm).

Obermann, C. E. 1965. A History of Vocational Rehabilitation in America (Minneapolis, MN: T. S. Denison).

Parsons, Talcott. 1956. "Suggestions for a Sociological Approach to the Theory of Organizations." Administrative Science Quarterly 1:225-39.

Perrow, C. 1963. "Goals and Power Structure: A Historical Case Study." In The Hospital in Modern Society, edited by E. Friedson (Chicago, IL: The Free Press of Glencoe), pp. 112-46.

_____. 1979. Complex Organizations, 2d ed. (Glencoe, IL: Scott, Foresman).

Pfeffer, Jeffrey. 1977. "The Ambiguity of Leadership." Academy of Management Review 2, no. 1:104-12.

_____. 1981. Power in Organizations (Marshfield, MA: Pitman).

Pfeffer, Jeffrey and G. Salancik. 1978. The External Control of Organizations (New York: Harper & Row).

Piaget, Jean. 1971. Structuralism (London: Routledge and Kegan Paul).

Quinn, J. B. 1977. "Strategic Goals: Process and Politics." Management Review 18:21-37.

Schendel, D., A. Cooper, and K. Hatten. 1978. "A Strategic Model of the U.S. Brewing Industry: 1952-1971." Academy of Management Journal 21:562-610.

Schendel, Dan and C. Hofer. 1979. Strategic Management (Boston, MA: Little, Brown).

Scott, R. A. 1967. "The Factory as a Social Service Organization: Goal Displacement in Workshops for the Blind." Social Problems 15:160-75.

Selznick, Philip. 1949. TVA and the Grass Roots (Berkeley, CA: University of California Press).

_____. 1957. Leadership in Administration (New York: Harper & Row).

Simon, Herbert. 1976. Administrative Behavior, 3d ed. (New York: The Free Press).

Smits, S. and J. Ledbetter. 1979. "The Practice of Rehabilitation Counseling Within the Administrative Structure of the State-Federal Program." Journal of Applied Rehabilitation Counselling 10, no. 2:78-84.

Starbuck, William. 1976. "Organizations and Their Environments." Handbook of Organizational and Industrial Psychology, edited by Marvin Dunnette (Chicago, IL: Rand-McNally), pp. 1069-1123.

Stava, Per. 1976. "Constraints on the Politics of Public Choice." In In Ambiguity and Choice in Organizations, edited by James March and J. Olsen (Bergen, Norway: Universitets Forlaget), pp. 206-24.

Stewart, Richard. 1975. "The Reformation of American Administrative Law." Harvard Law Review 88:1667-1813.

Stone, Katherine. 1974. "The Origins of Job Structure in the Steel Industry." Reprinted in Mary Zey-Ferrell and Michael Aiken, pp. 349-81.

Stopford, J. and L. Wells. 1972. Managing the Multinational Enterprise (New York: Basic Books).

Taijfel, Henri. 1969. "Social and Cultural Factors in Perception, Handbook of Social Psychology," vol. 3, edited by G. Lindzey and E. Aronson (Reading, MA: Addison Wesley).

Tannenbaum, A. S. 1968. Control in Organizations (New York: McGraw-Hill).

Thain, Donald. 1976. "Stages of Corporate Development." in Business Policy: Strategy Formation & Management Action, 2d ed., edited by W. Glueck (New York: McGraw-Hill), p. 248.

Thompson, James. 1967. Organizations in Action (New York: McGraw-Hill).

Vromen, Suzanne. 1983. "Perverse Effects: Merton Revisited." Book Review in Contemporary Sociology 12, no. 4:372-74.

Weber, Max. 1968. Economy and Society, 4th ed., edited by G. Roth and C. Wittich (New York: Irvington).

Weiss, Joseph. 1981. "The Historical and Political Perspective on Organizations of Lucien Karpik." In Mary Zey-Ferrell and M. Aiken, pp. 382-96.

Wessen, Albert. 1965. "The Apparatus of Rehabilitational Analysis." In Sociology and Rehabilitation, edited by Marvin B. Sussman (Washington, D.C.: American Sociological Association), pp. 141-63.

Whetten, D. 1980. "Organizational Decline: A Neglected Topic in Organizational Science." Academy of Management Review 5, no. 4:577-85.

Wildavsky, A. 1968. "Budgeting as a Political Process." In The International Encyclopedia of the Social Sciences, vol. 2, edited by David L. Sills (New York: Crowell, Collier and MacMillan), pp. 192-99.

____. 1979. The Politics of the Budgeting Process, 3d ed. (Boston, MA: Little, Brown).

Wright, George. 1980. Total Rehabilitation (Boston, MA: Little, Brown).

Zey-Ferrell, M. and M. Aiken. 1981. Complex Organizations. Critical Perspectives (Glenview, IL: Scott, Foresman).

Index

203

state VR administration, constraints on, 54-55
state vocational rehabilitation agencies, 54
strategic choice perspective, 9-19; examples of, 19
strategies, 16, 63; defining, 25-26; flexible, 111; during growth period, 60-109; identifying, 24; limitations and lessons, 187-188
structure, 111
systematic perspective, importance of, 11
Switzer, Mary E., 46, 47

Thain, Donald, 111
top-level management: coercive, 102; logics of power, 101; policy formation activities of, 39
training: for disabled clients, 74; vocational education staff, 44
transmission belt perspective, 107-108
turbulence: events and trends 1975-78, 112-116; national level, 113-114; resultant policies and logics of action, 131-136; at state and local level, 114-116; strategic responses to, 120-128; strategies during, 110-150

urban directors, 73-74; dissatisfaction with Adams' policies, 95; guaranteed income level, 87; position in strategies during growth, 85

validity, defined, 40
value orientation, 70
Vocational Educational Board, funding requests to, 64
Vocational Education program, 107
vocational rehabilitation, 33; vs. educational rehabilitation, 79; expenditure increases, 46; growth, 33; success and growth of, 82; success measurement statistics, 90-91
Vocational Rehabilitation, Office of, 45
Vocational Rehabilitation Act (1973), 124
vocational rehabilitation legislation: battle phase of, 48-50; Great Depression and, 45-46; great growth phase, 46
vulnerability, 112; factors contributing to, 113

Weberian bureaucracy, 107
work activities, defined, 57
workshop directors, cooperative agreements, 125
workshops, 46, 48; budget allocations, 56; competitive environment, 85-89; decreased dependence on for funding, 78; forced selectivity, 87; funds for construction of, 58; funds for staffing, 58; importance of to VR study, 57; underestimating pay rates in facilities, 88

zealots, 109, 110

About the Author

JOSEPH W. WEISS is an Assistant Professor of Management at Bentley College, Waltham, Massachusetts.

Dr. Weiss worked as an administrator with the states of Massachusetts and Wisconsin, and has consulted with several departments in these state governments. He has also supervised research and consulted with high-tech firms in New England.

Dr. Weiss has made presentations to the Academy of Management, the Midwest Business Association, and the American Sociological Association. He currently is researching the environmental and cultural differences between New England and Silicon Valley high-tech firms from CEO perspectives.

Dr. Weiss received his Ph.D. from the University of Wisconsin at Madison, specializing in industrial sociology and administrative science.